COMMANDERS

AMERICAN GENERALS FROM LEE TO SCHWARZKOPF

LENNART SVENSSON

MANTICORE PRESS

COMMANDERS

AMERICAN GENERALS FROM LEE TO SCHWARZKOPF

Lennart Svensson

© Manticore Press (Australia, 2018)

Thema Classification: NHW (Military History), JWL (War & Defence), 1KBB (United States of America), NHK (History of the Americas)

978-0-6482996-3-9

MANTICORE PRESS
WWW.MANTICORE.PRESS

CONTENTS

Introduction   5

1. Robert E. Lee (1807-1870)   9

2. George G. Meade (1815-1872)   19

3. U. S. Grant (1822-1885)   23

4. Thomas "Stonewall" Jackson (1824-1863)   39

5. George B. McClellan (1826-1885)   43

6. George A. Custer (1839-1876)   47

7. John J. Pershing (1861-1948)   55

8. George C. Marshall (1880-1959)   59

9. Douglas MacArthur (1880-1964)   63

10. George S. Patton (1885-1945)   73

11. Dwight D. Eisenhower (1893-1968)   85

12. Omar N. Bradley (1893-1981)   91

13. Claire Lee Chennault (1893-1958)   97

14. James H. Doolittle (1896-1993)   103

15. Leslie R. Groves (1896-1970)   111

16. Charles E. Yeager (1923-)   119

17. The Korean War   125

18. The Vietnam War   131

19. H. Norman Schwarzkopf (1934-2012)   139

20. Marginalia   153

Bibliographical Note   *169*

Literature   *171*

Index of Persons   *175*

About the Author   *177*

INTRODUCTION

THIS IS A COLLECTION OF STORIES, focused on generals of the United States of America. It is an historical survey focusing on operational and other warlike circumstances. In the process, I also share some anecdotes and cultural tidbits.

However, I won't go into *politics*. Not that I'm uninformed about it and that I don't know about the ins and outs of American (foreign) policy from the beginning until today. I know this and that. And I can be critical of what I'm officially told. Like I say in the chapter about Norman Schwarzkopf and the run-up to the Gulf War of 1990: I doubt the official American narrative of this event. Further, I can also add that I doubt the official American narrative of many other conflicts in its history. But, enough said of that, since I won't explore that perspective in this book. There will be no explicitly political deliberations, critiques, examinations, discussions, and preachments on these pages. Instead, what you'll get, from the Civil War to the Gulf War, are stories of the respective generals and pertinent facts of war, military operations, tactics and strategy, and a lot of other things I get the urge to mention as I go along.

As for a certain feature of the book, that of ignoring the War of Independence and starting directly with the Civil War, I know that there were noteworthy American generals around even in 1776. But, as a creative writer, these guys don't inspire me. For portraits of generals, I've decided to focus on the "battlefield hero" archetype. And the only figure approaching that in the War of Independence was Benedict Arnold (like, for instance, at Saratoga). But he later became a traitor. That doesn't inspire me. So, the beginnings were difficult in this case – the case of having a sufficiently inspirational era to start with. Instead, I felt more inspired to start with Robert E. Lee and the Civil War. When I read and write about war, there must be a certain *flow* involved, a certain level of operations, a certain amount of "big unit maneuver warfare". There must be a broad canvas to paint on and the Civil War and subsequent wars in this book provided me with that. The War of Independence didn't.

You might say that the Vietnam War lacks this "big unit warfare" quality, and I admit that. However, that war interests me on other levels, which is why it's included. The Vietnam War was a major focus of interest for my generation, covering it was a requirement.

The focus of the book is on battlefields and armies, on the *US Army* proper. Also, three portraits of Air Force generals are included (Chennault, Doolittle, and Yeager) – and war in the air isn't about battlefield action, it's an airspace business. However, all the airmen portrayed started their careers in the US Army, the air force branch of it only becoming an independent service arm in 1947. For their part, *US Navy* and sea battles are pretty much left out of the book, the naval side of things only covered in a section in Chapter 20, "Marginalia".

The formal structure of the book is this: *a collection of biographical portraits*. The historically oldest general (Lee) comes first, then the next oldest etc. This "collection of portraits" structure could mean some repetition—but—when writing the chapters, at all times I have had an eye on the shape of the big picture. I've wanted to give the reader "a good read," a book that (theoretically) could be read from start to finish, as a kind of implicit history of the US at war.

Structural details aside, you could say that I've tried to write a serious essay in popular form.

Or, you could say that these are war stories, told by the fireside with a glass of whiskey in the hand...

Härnösand, Sweden, 1 August 2018

LENNART SVENSSON

1. ROBERT E. LEE (1807-1870)

HOW ABOUT THIS FOR DRAMA: the enemy is approaching the capital with an enormous army and a new general is called in to rectify the situation. And, in a seven-day battle, he pushes the enemy back, the attacker is chased away and retreats – the capital and the country is saved...!

This is exactly what happened outside of Richmond, Virginia, in the summer of 1862. The Civil War had been going on for over a year. The Confederate states had broken out of the Union and they had won a symbolic victory at the river Bull Run in Virginia, in July 1861, scattering the Union force. But now the Union General McClellan approached with a professionally organized army, *the Army of the Potomac,* with maintenance and reserves in place and a rather ingenious plan to operate by. "Little Mac" he was called, this General-in-Chief of the Union, George Brinton McClellan, and he aimed at attacking the capital of the Confederacy from the south, starting from the coast after an amphibious landing. Thus, he didn't have to advance through the poorly mapped forests and thickets of the shortest distance between Washington and Richmond.

The army boarded the transport ships, sailed away and landed on the Yorktown peninsula, known from the Revolutionary War; the final battle that time, ending with a rebel victory, was the siege of Yorktown. The thrust toward Richmond began and the Confederate G-i-C, Joseph E. Johnston, was wounded. Then, Confederate President Jefferson Davis came to think of *Robert Edward Lee,* having hitherto only been an advisor and a somewhat indolent commander in western Virginia. Apart from having had a long, distinguished career in the peacetime army, Lee lacked the ability to fire people; he had a gentlemanly leadership style which also came to characterize his subsequent generalship – for better or worse.

Lee was given command of the main army of the Confederacy and now things really got off the ground. In June, Mac had reached the vicinities of Richmond, the Confederate capital, but his northern flank was rather exposed and Lee began to plan an attack against this. He went out into the field and ordered a counter-attack, and thus began what came to be known as the Seven Days Battle.

***

On the first day of battle, something unexpected happened: Mac attacked! But it was only a probing attack and the Confederates held their positions. The next day was also about to go badly for the Confederacy for their skilled General Thomas "Stonewall" Jackson didn't arrive in time at his allotted place in the formation. It was in the Mechanicsville region and the situation was saved by another of Lee's corps attacking, storming forward in their grey uniforms and chasing away the Yankees in their traditional dark blue uniforms. The Confederacy carried the day but had high losses, as was the rule in this war: the usual attacks of the traditional, "storming ahead with a leveled bayonet" kind were costly, something that the generals only slowly learned. The new, rifled guns had a longer range of fire than the muskets previously used, 6-700 to 1-200 meters. This made storming attacks over open fields into pure shooting exercises for the defender.

Lee had started to dig into Mac's northern flank. The latter realized this and retreated quite orderly, even to the last day of the battle, 1 July. For instance, looking at day three of the campaign, on June 27, it was a clear-cut success for the South: Jackson was finally in place and the Union defensive line was broken through. However, even when he had arrived at Richmond Jackson didn't advance very quickly, but this may have been due to poor maps. Even if this was friendly territory the terrain had a pattern of small woods, fields, and meadows which hadn't been adequately mapped. For instance, white spots could be fields or they could be swamps – which would be fatal.

The battle continued and McClellan retreated orderly, he was never cut off, which was a feat of itself. Lee had wanted to encircle him to end the war in one big *coup the main,* a *Vernichtungsschlacht* à la Schlieffen, but no general succeeded in this during the main course of the war. Perhaps the greatest chance was with Meade after Gettysburg, as we shall see later. Otherwise, the Civil War was a succession of what Schlieffen called *ordinary victories:* although one side "has won" (held the battlefield, had fewer casualties, etc.) neither side was routed, they both lived to fight another day.

On the last day of the Seven Days, Mac grouped on Malvern Hill and Lee couldn't drive him off this site. Costly attacks were made but contained. Losses were great for Lee and had been heavy all week, but the campaign as a whole was celebrated as a victory of the Confederacy. When it began, the enemy stood just outside of the capital with a well-equipped army, and when it ended, he was chased 40 km away, licking his wounds. Mac's army was finally shipped home bit by bit, and finally, he was deprived of command of it. But he would meet with Lee on the battlefield again.

***

Robert Edward Lee was born in Virginia in 1807. He chose the warrior's way like his father, graduating as second in line from West Point and choosing the Engineer Corps as service branch, the undisputed elite of those times. In the Mexican War, he served on the army HQ and as a recce officer, and later he was head of West Point for a while, the War Academy. In the late 1850s, he captured John Brown, a rebel who wanted to abolish slavery, occupying the arsenal Harper's Ferry for this purpose. But the whole attempt was quelled and Brown was executed for conspiracy – and they made a

11

song about him, the one which became the number one fight song for the Union, "*Battle Hymn of the Republic*":

John Brown's body lies a-mouldering in the grave,
his soul is marching on...

At the outbreak of war in 1861, President Lincoln offered Lee the command over the Union army. Lee declined. He primarily saw himself as a Virginian – and, since Virginia had chosen to secede and join the Confederacy, he had to go with it. He didn't want to fight against his children, he said. Otherwise, he considered secession a dubious principle, the right of states to secede was not vindicated by him *per se*. But, being a soldier, he didn't have to trouble his mind with these kinds of deliberations. He went to war with a clear consciousness. You might call it *implicit nationalism,* to fight for your own land.

Lee's father had served George Washington as a cavalry officer, having become known as "Light Horse Harry Lee". His wife Mary Custis was nothing less than the daughter of Washington's adopted son, George Washington Parke Custis. If we add to this that Lee was born in Virginia's Westmoreland County where Washington, too, had seen the light of day, you can understand that Lee appeared as something of an heir to Washington. The Confederacy, of course, played on these strings of propaganda: they were rebels like the freedom fighters of 1776, now fighting against the oppression of the Northern states.

After the Seven Days Battle, Lee became a hero and now began the *annus mirabilis* of the Confederacy, a year of victories. The main army was renamed "the Army of Northern Virginia," led by Lee and divided into two corps, commanded by Stonewall Jackson and James Longstreet respectively. The former was the heat, the latter the cold, and in between was Lee a balancing factor. This was a fine army but it would not suffice for victory, as the Union had larger reserves of men and a more diversified industry. But the contest certainly hung in the balance for a while.

After an easy victory against Pope (the Second Battle of Bull Run) Lee decided to invade Maryland, a slave state in the Union. The goal was to enlist recruits for the Confederacy, perhaps enlist the entire state to its cause, but also to loot supplies. For instance, Lee's army suffered from a lack of shoes. The march into Maryland was not to be triumphal, the state remained in the Union, and operationally it was about to go awry when a written order fell into the hands of the enemy.

Union commander was now again McClellan. He read the intercepted order but didn't act on it immediately, being slow as usual, rendering the gained information useless. Meanwhile, Lee retreated to the town of Sharpsburg, deploying the army in a distribution going from north to south between the city and the river Antietam Creek. So, what would Mac do? As intimated, attacking against prepared positions was difficult during this war, harder than before, but Mac planned to attack gradually in the north, center, and south; the whole line would be involved so that reinforcements couldn't be sent between the different parts.

Such was the plan and it was put into effect on 17 September 1862. However, delays on the Union side enabled Lee to meet and contain the attacks one by one. It all became something of a slaughter – for both sides. The Battle of Antietam was the bloodiest day of the war, it is said, upwards of 60,000 are said to have died. Lee lost a quarter of his entire army, but afterward he could retreat to Virginia and count the whole affair as a defensive victory. President Lincoln also thought that the whole thing had been a decent success, making it the basis for his first announcement of slave emancipation. The final Emancipation Act was issued at the beginning of 1863.

For Mac, however, the war was over, Lincoln disliking the fact that he hadn't pursued Lee after the battle. Certainly, McClellan was a bit slow, and he never won a clear victory. He wasn't a great general, but he was a steady workman and he built the Union army into an instrument that could endure the command even of mediocre generals. Now, for example, followed Burnside, who was defeated at Fredericksburg after an unimaginative frontal assault. His successor

"Fighting Joe" Hooker was better. However, at Chancellorsville, in April 1863, Lee thought he could outflank him by sending out Jackson's corps in a circumventing movement.

Jackson was undeniably a born warrior, an intuitive general who out performed many "political" Union generals in the Shenandoah Valley before he became Lee's corps commander. But we don't know if he was the best general of the war, and we won't speculate on what would have happened if he hadn't fallen, mistakenly fired at by blue force troops during the Battle of Chancellorsville.

What we do know is that the battle was fought in rather forested terrain, where overview and cohesion were difficult. But thanks to the forest terrain Jackson also managed to move his troops in a concealed fashion, and he really did attack Hooker in the flank and surprise him. Then, Jackson himself was lethally injured after a recce ride – but, the confusion was great on the Union side too, and Hooker was already in a state of retreat. Hooker himself was hit by a falling beam from a front porch hit by artillery; the general became somewhat groggy and could only order a retreat.

Lee grieved over Jackson's death but otherwise everything after Chancellorsville spoke for the Confederacy. It was believed to be riding a wave of victory; it was now or never, it had to risk a decisive battle, march north and strike at the Union once and for all.

Lee had led his forces to victory at Chancellorsville. Everything looked rosy; now was the time for a decisive battle, a *coup de main* that would determine the war, a *Vernichtungsschlacht* having the great powers recognize the Confederacy as a sovereign state. The Confederates had a year of success, seeing themselves as freedom fighters with the right on their side. Also, they had no choice but to dare this great venture because they suffered from the Union naval blockade and lacked the resources of the Union.

The battle trumpet was blown and the forces were gathered, and Lee mounted his trusty steed Traveler and marched north this summer of 1863. The *general direction* was Washington but the *primary target* was the enemy army. In early July the two contesting forces finally met in the region of Gettysburg, Pennsylvania. Now the North had the advantage that Lee had at Sharpsburg and Fredericksburg, a prepared defensive position. Lee must attack Meade's long line on Cemetery Ridge, and this failed. But he had no choice, he must dare an attack, because without an attack an enemy can't be defeated.

In this era, the master of the battlefield was a kind of rifle, muzzle-loaded but with a rifled barrel. However, generals like Lee didn't quite get this, they still had the bayonet charge dominating their "tactical subconscious," this would determine every battle they fought. So, having tried and failed to attack the flanks of Meade's position there was nothing else to do than attacking in the center, a move known to posterity as "Pickett's Charge" after the brigade commander in question. It was the culmination of the battle as well as of the sequence of Confederate victories; the last "rebel yell," now marching steadily against a hail of bullets and grapeshot, the hostile fire thinning out the lines even though a few scattered units reached the top of the hill waving the Stars and Bars – and then retreat and defeat.

Besides the unimaginative master plan, you might see Lees gentlemanly leadership as contributing to the defeat. As was sometimes the case in Lee's battles, what was missing was a firm hand. His orders never read, "take the village or die," but more like, "if it's possible, can you take the village"... Then you might object and say that all American generals have been rather gentlemanly, this isn't Soviet Russia, but to this I say, MacArthur in the Pacific War could give tough orders, like the one to Eichelberg on New Guinea ordering him to take Buna "or not come back alive". And Patton in Tunisia 1943 ordering a long-serving general to personally lead an assault on a hill, a battle in which the general—Orlando Ward—was wounded in the eye. So, details aside, a firm hand is needed in battle command. A soldier can't always be a gentleman.

The Gettysburg battlefield is nowadays a scenic location, well suited to tourism and philosophical wanderings. A man having wandered around there is Kent Gramm, so those who like to bother their minds over the "why" and "how could it happen" of the Civil

War are recommended to read his *Gettysburg: A Meditation on War and Values* (1998). A philosophical outing, a deliberation on "the trauma of war" which is real and of course shouldn't be denied. The Civil War to an American probably is what WWI is to a European: a major crisis, a cataclysm ending a golden age. Otherwise, in the realm of stylish Civil War accounts, we rather recommend Carl Sandburg's *Storm Over the Land*. A linear narrative from the beginning of the war to its end, this story has a wealth of telling detail, like the words of the dying boy soldier after Bull Run: "It grows very dark, mother, very dark"...

***

As for the Battle of Gettysburg it turned into a decisive Confederate defeat. However, in the middle of misery Lee didn't lose his mind; he took responsibility for the whole thing and kept a level head, gathering his army to an orderly retreat and escaping from the claws of the enemy. The Union commander George Meade was a cautious general who didn't dare pursue, he had won a tactical victory and was happy with it. Lincoln, of course, insisted on relentless pursuit but to no avail. Formally, Lincoln was right to demand this, "the war might have been ended in an afternoon" by way of an active chase and harassment of the weak remains of the Army of Northern Virginia. Then again, you never know, because the terrain in question wasn't a level, open field, it was "broken" with clearings alternating with woods which in this tactical case might have favored the Confederacy.

In any case, the Confederates marched home and under Lee continued to do battle for another two years. Now Lee had to face U. S. Grant, a more unrelenting and persistent commander than anyone he had previously met on the battlefield. Details aside, Grant knew that unconditional surrender was the only option; any other goal would prolong the conflict indefinitely. Again, details and "who was right" aside, the smallest concession to the South would have meant a recognition of them as an independent state, the approval of secession as a principle, and this wasn't what Grant and Lincoln had in mind. Lincoln only fought for the preservation of the Union, no half measures, and Grant was his firm ally in this.

Lee and Grant now fought against each other in Virginia, meeting in various battles in the spring of 1864, most having the character of monotonous hammerings. Lee warded off the blows and kept his flanks secure—but—in the back, he had the Union general Sherman advancing on him. A continental strategy was finally working, the pressure would be constant, Lee wouldn't be able to send reserves to the point for the moment being threatened. Operationally, he would be denied the benefit of the internal lines.

This was a successful strategy, for in the spring of 1865 Lee was forced to give up the defenses in front of Richmond where stationary, "siege-type" trench battles had been going on since the summer of 1864. Now, Lee thought of marching west to join Johnston who fought against Sherman somewhere in North Carolina. But it was far away and on the way, Lee's column was harried by numerous Union cavalry. Then it became quiet for a few days – but it was only because Grant was about to bypass and encircle the remains of the Army of Northern Virginia, once counting 80,000 men and now only having about 9,000 left.

Grant succeeded with his movement, Lee was encircled and realized that everything was over. He asked to see Grant to surrender, which came to be in the Appomattox Court House. This took place in April 1865. The Civil War had ended and the Union was restored.

Lee was perhaps not the greatest general ever, he gave his subordinates a bit too much freedom. He was a bit too gentlemanly for mortal combat. And Gettysburg was a resounding defeat. But he was a brilliant tactician who won many stylish victories. And he had charisma, almost royal charisma if you ask me. He was long and tall, had grey hair and a full beard; the only thing that disturbed the picture was possibly his somewhat small feet. Furthermore, he disliked public speaking, but this is perhaps in itself a royal trait; an aristocrat is primarily supposed to rule by charisma and character, not by convincing the opponent of his opinion in a pointed speech like some demagogue.

After the defeat, Lee worked as a school teacher, becoming through his whole being a worthy representative of a beaten people. He didn't look like a broken man, refusing to play the role of a loser. He also said that there was no need to be ashamed, the Confederacy had fought for something they believed in – for the Southern lifestyle, Southern nationalism.

Details aside, in the time of defeat the Southerners were strengthened by Lee's example. He showed them how to accept *fait accompli* without fretting.

2. GEORGE G. MEADE (1815-1872)

LET'S TALK A LITTLE ABOUT *Civil War weapons* and *the tactics* these implied.

The most important new item in this war was the rifled handgun, the name implying the rifles of the barrel, giving the fired bullet rotation and therefore a more stable, longer trajectory compared to a bullet fired with a smooth-bore musket. The old-school musket had a range of about 100 meters, the new gun about 700 meters. Even better guns were back-loaded bolt-action ones but these mainly came after the war, the Civil War rifle still being muzzle-loaded.

During the era of the musket, an attacker could feel secure up to 100 meters away from the enemy. And this was also the maximum range of fire of his own handguns. Then, there would be an exchange of fire and then the attacker would advance with the bayonet. And take the enemy position? Not always, the defense is always stronger than the attack, and in the equation, there was also artillery and cavalry shocks. But overall, in this era attacks were comparatively simple; it was rather rational to launch them. They had a fine chance of succeeding.

This changed with the arrival of the rifle. An attacker was now exposed to defensive, small-caliber fire during a much longer time than before. Civil War generals didn't understand this, they went on as in the Napoleonic period, marching in closed order against the enemy with the result that the soldiers would be shot down one by one. The defender could fire salvo after salvo and still feel rather safe that the attacker wouldn't reach storming distance. Of course, there were exceptions to this rule, old-school storming attacks could succeed, but in general, the latter half of the 19th century meant a new era in army tactics. As for artillery, it was still around but it was vulnerable; the range of a smooth-bore cannon was about 500 meters and thus the services on the battlefield could be exposed to rifle fire, range 700 meters. As for cavalry in America, its role was marginal in the Revolutionary War and in the Civil War it had the character of mounted infantry along with being useful for patrols and raids. There was no room for old-school cavalry shocks in the main battle environment, for half of the troopers would be shot down before they were at "chopping distance" with their sabers.

Civil War generals didn't always get this. Their tactical subconscious was Napoleonic. But by the end of the war, the lessons began to be learned, like allowing infantry to take successive cover during attacks. However, it should be remembered that a muzzle-loader was easier to load standing up, the force of gravity thus helping to drive the bullet down the barrel.

***

The focus of interest for this chapter is *George Gordon Meade* who was born in 1815 as the son of an American ship broker in Cadiz, Spain. After West Point graduation in 1835, Meade inter alia participated in the fighting against the Seminole Indians in Florida and in the Mexican War. In the latter, he was promoted First Lieutenant for brave conduct.

After the war, Meade built lighthouses in Florida. In August 1861, he was promoted Brigadier General and placed in the Army of the Potomac, where he came to serve the entire war. Up and until Gettysburg he took part in most of its battles as brigade or division commander, apart from when he was recuperating after an injury received in the Seven Days Battle of 1862.

Eventually, Meade became the head of the Army of the Potomac. It was early in the morning on 28 June 1863. A rider arrived at a camp in Maryland with a message from Washington. It was an order to general Meade; the tent in question was found and Meade was awakened. The messenger said that he was there to bring him trouble but Meade just said that he had a clear conscience, received the message and read it. It was from Henry Halleck, chief of staff in Washington who said that on the order of the President you are hereby appointed the head of the Army of the Potomac. Furthermore, it was said that Meade was given a free hand to lead the operations, "you will not be hampered by any minute instructions from headquarters; your army is free to act as you may deem proper under the circumstances as they arise."

This was a sound order, giving the commander free hands. Now Lee was in the vicinities, he might have had Washington as a goal but he must defeat the Union army first – and this lead to a northern detour, ending in Gettysburg, Pennsylvania, the northernmost battlefield of the war. Meade installed himself in a strong defensive position on a ridge, *Cemetery Ridge,* a ridge about 12 meters high. Meade knew that now it was about standing or falling; for this matter, he for instance placed out troopers armed with carbines behind the line ensuring that no Union soldier left his place during the fight. The ensuing battle again proved the strength of the defense of this war, like the Battle of Fredericksburg in reverse; then, in December 1862, the Union had attacked in vain against a Confederate wall of lead. Now the Confederates were to experience the same.

Lee lost the battle and had to retreat. Meade didn't pursue but it would have been comparatively easy to do that; Lee's army was weakened and demoralized and could have been encircled and eradicated, ending the war there and then, but Meade, a cautious general, was satisfied with his victory. He had a free hand to do whatever he pleased, and thus he didn't listen to Lincoln's prayers to pursue Lee.

Lincoln wasn't so glad of this lethargy of Meade, it was like McClellan all over again. However, Meade remained in command of the Army of the Potomac—but—with U. S. Grant as General-in-Chief making all the strategic decisions.

After the surrender of the Confederacy in 1865, the South was forcibly occupied by the Union, installing a kind of military rule, seeing to it that a rebellion didn't break out again. Meade was part of that regime, serving as military governor of the district of Georgia-Alabama-Florida for several years. For instance, he made an effort to allow Georgia to be reinstated in the Union in 1868, but it was delayed. Not until July 1870 was that state allowed to re-enter, with full rights, except for the right to secede, in the United States of America. On the whole, the occupation of the South went on to 1877, at least formally. Regarding for example West Point, the War Academy of the Republic, it only began to allow southern cadets in the 1880s.

3. U. S. GRANT (1822-1885)

ULYSSES SIMPSON GRANT WAS BORN IN 1822 in Ohio as the son of Jesse House Grant. When Ulysses was eight years old, the father sent him to buy a horse from a certain Mr. Ralston. Ralston had set the price to 25 dollars but Jesse thought that the animal wasn't worth more than 20 dollars. The father said to his son to offer this sum, with an option to go to 22 ½, and if this didn't work, go to 25. So young Grant went to Ralston and said:

> "Dad says that I can give you 20 bucks for the horse, but if you don't accept that I can give you 22 ½, and if you don't accept that I can give you 25..."

The father wanted the son to become a tanner like him, but, when Ulysses refused, he sent him to West Point. He was registered as *Ulysses Simpson Grant,* the middle name being the maternal family name. Grant didn't much enjoy West Point and he later said that when he left it was the happiest day of his life. He stood out only in horse riding; overall his grades were mediocre and therefore he was commissioned to the infantry. He served in obscurity in the 4th Regiment until he was called out in *the Mexican War* where he became a bold striker and quartermaster. When he met Lee at the capitulation 1865 the latter said that he remembered him from this time, which Grant noted with some pride in his memoirs.

Grant's career before the Civil War was rather dismal. Having reached the rank of Captain he soon had to resign because of drunkenness; he was the type of man who became intoxicated by the slightest intake of alcohol. Next, he got a livelihood for his family on a farm procured by his father-in-law, a Southerner named Dent, but this didn't go so well. Shortly before the war Grant was paymaster in the tannery his father and his brothers, had located in a burgh by the name of Galena, Illinois.

It was a day in the spring of 1861. Grant, as always looking a bit unkempt, was sitting on an empty crate in front of the leather business. By this time some southern states had seceded and, here in the North, patriotism ran high in defense of the Union. One businessman in Galena had set up a voluntary company and this day it was exercising in front of Grant's facility. But the businessman gave an incorrect command and the ranks became disordered. Then the commander caught sight of Grant sitting there dozing in the sun – Grant, whom he knew had been a captain in the regular army. So, he asked him to take command of the company and gave him his sword. And when Grant put the sword-belt on and presented arms before the company, he was transformed – because here, a witness said, you saw a man who knew something about martial exercise and associated subjects.

Soon Grant enlisted in the voluntary army which was set up to defend the Union; the regular army continued with its duties of defending the borders and patrolling the plains. Grant received command of the 21st Illinois Infantry Regiment, an unruly unit whose previous manager mostly held speeches and took his sentinels out for a drink in the evening. When Grant was presented to his new troop and was asked to hold a speech, he just said:

"Go to your quarters!"

The regiment was broken in and immediately sent to northern Missouri, a state vacillating between the northern and southern camp. An expedition would be carried out against a hostile force under one Colonel Harris; Grant was the chief at this point, he was the one in charge for his unit, but the more he approached Harris' presumed grouping the more he wished that he was only a major without the overall responsibility. When he came to the suspected spot, however, Harris had fallen back, proving that he had also been afraid... Grant duly took note of this psychological fact of warfare – that it's a duel, even when it comes to perceptions and expectations. It's a war of nerves, of wills.

After this episode, Grant was promoted Brigadier General, soon to become head of all troops in southern Illinois and southeast Missouri, with headquarters in Cairo near the confluence of the Ohio and the Mississippi Rivers. The important point Paducah, by the Tennessee River outflow in Ohio, was occupied by Grant and subsequently, in November 1861, he operated against Belmont a bit downstream of the Mississippi. At Belmont Grant engaged the Confederate General Polk. Grant's men at first had some success and then being driven back to the boats having shipped them there, beating a not so honorable retreat.

**

The next big event in Grant's career were *the operations against Fort Henry and Fort Donelson*. As for the terrain, the two tributaries of the Ohio River were the Tennessee and Cumberland Rivers, flowing into the Ohio from the south. In their lower courses, they ran in parallel a short distance from each other; the latter was navigable up to Nashville in Kentucky, the latter a healthy bit down into Alabama, thus forming fine inroads to the Confederate area. General Polk had realized this and built fortifications at each river, in a region where the distance between the waters was only 20 km. Grant now wanted to attack these, first Fort Henry and then Fort Donelson, which he at long last was allowed to do; cannon boats would be sent down the Tennessee River while Grant himself attacked Fort Henry over land with 15,000 men. Fort Henry was situated on the east side of the Tennessee River, a large defense establishment, four hectares wide. On the other side of the river, the western, it was covered by a semi-finished outpost; on the eastern riverside the main fort was defended by high terrain and seventeen guns. The night of 5 and 6 February

25

1862 the outpost—Fort Heiman—was taken; it wasn't in use. The next day at 11 o'clock Fort Henry was to be taken and its garrison captured so that it couldn't reinforce Fort Donelson, the next target.

Grant saw to it that the gunboats with their fifty pieces began to bombard the fortress, advancing about 300 meters from the fort whereby the "red force" cannons were silenced. The commander of the fort saw that the whole affair was going badly for him so he ordered an evacuation to Fort Donelson, which to a large extent succeeded. He himself stayed behind and surrendered at 2 o'clock in the afternoon.

This was rather easy: the cannon boats subdued the fortress, Grant didn't need to deploy the ground troops he had with him. In the next operation, it would be different; Fort Donelson, situated 20 km east of Fort Henry on the west side of the Cumberland River, was ten times as large as Fort Henry and was located on a 30 meter height. Furthermore, it was protected by bastions or gun emplacements and two minor water courses, Hickman Creek in the north and the Indian Creek in the south, which both flowed into the Cumberland River. To the west and south the fort was protected by a string of posts with gun pits, and inside the fort were several pieces with fields of fire both toward the river and the terrain.

In addition to this fortress, the Confederates had an army deployed in the region, led by the Texan Albert Sidney Johnston. According to Fuller, he could have gone with his army to the fortress' proximity to constitute a movable reserve, which would have deterred Grant from attack. He could also simply have attacked Grant. Instead, he chose to reinforce the fortress garrison. It is believed that Johnston was shocked by the quick fall of Fort Henry; the cannon boats seemed to be such a first-class threat that normal rules for battle didn't apply. Now he had made a half-measure, detailing half of his army to man Donelson, in the hope that the garrison would hold out for as long as possible and then break out, while the remaining half were kept loitering in Nashville with him. He was at odds with the old wisdom: *Hold on to a strong reserve! Don't squander! Strike!*

Grant's idea, for its part, was to go against Donelson as quickly as possible, regardless of the odds. Better to attack with 15,000 now instead of with 50,000 after a month, was the idea, thus, a variant of the Napoleonic *Vitesse, Vitesse, de l'activité.* The fortress would be contained from the land side while the dear cannon boats, on the way from Fort Henry via the Tennessee and the Ohio and down the Cumberland River, would decide the affair and break the fortress. After a march through mud and pouring rain Grant deployed with two divisions to the west of the fortress, between the creeks and outside of the post chain, as well as two divisions in the east. It was February and cold and wet; usually armies didn't operate in winter, this was a time to be quartered and rest, but Grant was no traditional general, he would press on regardless and get things done. And in this case, deciding to march on Donelson right away, proved to be a correct estimation of the situation.

On 13 February the cannon boats arrived. They began pelting the defenses but the results were meager, the fort defended itself and the fleet had to retreat the way it had come with many boats damaged. But despite the success, the fortress commander was shocked by the whole affair; he decided to abandon the fortress, make a breakout toward Nashville and the main force of Johnston. On 15 February, the Union troops in the south were driven back by a sally from the fort; now the Confederates had a chance to get away, the Grant lines were disorganized – but the garrison hadn't prepared itself to break out, like rations not having been distributed and a rearguard not having been detailed. The commander of the vanguard became confused and ordered a retreat, and soon it was back in the fort. Grant had been away when this commotion began, visiting the gunboat commander; on returning he is said to have lost his wits for a moment—but—then he straightened up and commanded the troops in the south to retreat beyond the range of the cannons and dig in, and he sent a courier to the gunboat commander to make a demonstration against the fortress. Then he ordered a general advance of all ground forces; Grant had the feeling that the enemy was demoralized, even if his own troops also were a little shaky because of the unexpected breakout attempt – so the affair was now gloriously undecided and the first commander who shaped up and acted would win the battle. Grant understood this so he whipped up the morale of his unit, giving it renewed vigor; for example, the divisions in the west got going quickly, advancing on the fort. The chain of Confederate posts was broken through, by battalions, the Union moved closer, met by defensive rifle fire, nonetheless succeeding in taking a corner of the fort – a great success.

The attackers spent the night in this distribution, overnighting in the open air. At the same time in the garrison, a war council was held. The command of the fort was successively handed down to finish in the hands of the youngest general, while the two senior generals fled in the dark with 3,000 men.

Buckner was the name of the hapless general left to commandeer the wreck. Now he began to parley with Grant, he said he wanted to hear the conditions of the capitulation, but Grant only said:

No terms except unconditional surrender can be accepted. I propose to move immediately upon your works. I am, Sir, very respectfully your obedient servant, U. S. Grant, Brigadier General Commanding.

Buckner thought this was ungentlemanly; he might have expected something like the old-school "freely marching out with flying colors," but he had no choice and soon surrendered with 12,000 men and forty cannons. Grant, for his part, was operationally right in requesting submission; generals in the field by this time had a tendency to act on their own accord, like Sherman who negotiated a generous capitulation in 1865 (one which was later withdrawn because it lacked the support of Lincoln). Details aside, Grant understood that they were involved in a total war and that only capitulation would be possible. The Union public opinion was glad of this victory, it was the first real success for their arms in the war and the "US" of Grant's name was interpreted as "unconditional surrender" by a clever journalist. In a wider sense, the battle meant

LENNART SVENSSON

that Missouri and Kentucky were won over to the Union side and that Tennessee lay open for invasion.

Grant was promoted Major General and advanced further down the Tennessee River. On 6 and 7 April, he fought the battle of *Shiloh* where he had five divisions counting a total of 30,000 men grouped for defense, facing east and with the flank protected by rivers. He waited for reinforcements to be able to attack the Confederates in the node of Corinth, one day's march away. However, Grant was now surprised by the Confederates; the earlier mentioned Albert Sidney Johnston launched a surprise attack in the dawn of April 6 with 40,000. In addition to Grant in his naivety not expecting an attack the terrain was wooded, perfect terrain for such an assault, the woodland concealing the approach.

Grant was taken by surprise, he was driven back and his camp was conquered. Two divisions were routed and even in the afternoon, the Confederates seemed to have momentum left. By then, however, Johnston had fallen and General Beauregard had taken over. At the same time, Grant stood firm and waited for the darkness. He had the help of William Tecumseh Sherman in managing this difficult situation, Sherman having seen to it that it didn't evolve into a total Union defeat.

The next day, with reinforcements arrived, the Union side went to the attack, the Confederates gave ground and so it was over – for, there wasn't any pursuit phase, it seldom was during the Civil War. A general having won a battle was satisfied with holding the battleground, the retreating enemy was pretty much left alone and not harassed during a chase, with Meade after Gettysburg as the most fatal example of this syndrome of laziness. Grant's losses at Shiloh were 12,000 against the enemy's 9,000, which made this into one of the bloodiest battles in the West. Grant had been tactically surprised because of poor reconnaissance, poor defensive works and because he had his HQ 10 km away from his troops, for indeed, he was at this HQ when Johnston attacked. He is also said to have been surprised by the fury of the attack, that the Confederates attacked with such elemental force; he might have lived in the illusion that the war would soon be over but the dawn at Shiloh thwarted all his hopes of an imminent peace. Grant won the battle but in the short term his reputation was tarnished by it, some Union operators hinting that he had been drunk when he was surprised, and indeed he was relieved of command. But Lincoln saw through it all and kept believing in him, now or some other time saying of Grant: "I can't spare this man – he fights."

A rather odd Union general, Henry Halleck, took over the field army to march it to Corinth. He went methodically about, marching slowly, infinitely slowly, like a parody of the concept "a cautious general". No shots were fired and the enemy duly retreated before this force of 100,000, Halleck eventually marching into an abandoned city. For this, he was appointed to a newly created position, *General-in-Chief,* Union army commander just below the president, but in reality, this was mostly a title, a position of a glorified staff clerk. Halleck was indeed a great no-no, a man without originality, soldiery demeanor, and everything. In the process, Grant gained Western Tennessee as his military district, his first self-standing army command. Some minor battles were fought and won, all being a sort of run-up to the great campaign of *Vicksburg* on the eastern side of the Mississippi River in the late autumn of 1862. This was the Confederates' only remaining support at this river – so, if it was taken, the Confederation would be cut off from the granaries of Texas and Arkansas. But Vicksburg was a large, difficult fortress to take, impossible to attack from the north which would be logical since the ground was firm in that direction, the southern and eastern approaches being marshy. However, Grant chose to go by the latter way, "the bayou routes"; with a bold motion he left his base and let the men live on the hardtack and salted pork they could carry, making a bypass via marshland and bayou lakes to finally appear on the eastern side of the fortress. It was a feat having operated in this way, with 40,000 men cut off from their base – and the overall purpose, to surprise the enemy, was also achieved. The army approached the fortress from the east to besiege it, at the same time holding a relieving Confederate army at bay. The fortress was starved into submission and on 4 July, the National Day of 1863, it surrendered with 25,000 men and 170 cannons. Now any remaining doubts concerning Grant were nullified; first, after Donelson he had been relieved of command for a while, and also after Shiloh, but after Vicksburg the lament expired, Lincoln in him beginning to see the savior of the Union, symbolized in Grant being appointed G-i-C of the West with command over all the troops between the Mississippi and the Alleghenies.

At the same time as Vicksburg a campaign had been fought in Tennessee, and eventually was taken the railway node *Chattanooga* by the Union General Rosecrans. After the battle, he pursued the Confederate General Braxton Bragg, he thought he was completely shattered – but Bragg held his own and delivered battle in September at *Chickamauga,* Indian for "River of Blood". Rosecrans was saved by a certain General Thomas, "The Rock of Chickamauga". For his part, Thomas was a Southerner by birth but he felt obliged to fight on the Union side; at the outbreak of war, weighing the argument *pro et contra*, he could personally only decide that rebellion was wrong. His southern background worked against him career-wise, he never got an independent army command, the authorities probably suspecting him of going rebel and going over to the enemy with the army and everything. That was the spirit of the times, or in other words: it was *nationalism* brewing under the surface, clouded in words like "unique lifestyle" or the technicalities of secession.

Rosecrans retreated to Chattanooga. But those who know say that he retreated too far, in the process also abandoning the *Lookout Mountain* which dominated the city. With this out of reach the entire city should have been abandoned – for now, the Union force was in an unsatisfactory distribution, plagued by bad autumn weather and besieged by the enemy. Grant was summoned to the place to rectify the situation. He arrived on 23 October—'*wet, dirty, and well*' he wrote to Washington—and first saw to it to arrange the supplies for the three armies being grouped in Chattanooga. They were on the brink of starvation. After some reconnaissance, Grant decided on *a classic double envelopment*: the center army would bind the enemy in the front while the wings would turn 90 degrees and attack the enemy flanks. It happened to be that there were *two* hills on the location, both held by the Confederates, the prominent *Lookout Mountain* and then *Missionary Ridge* further back from where all which the Union did was observed. The Confederates could absorb each shock, reserves could be sent to the threatened areas.

In any case, on 23 November Sherman advanced towards the northern flank but when night came he halted. Maybe it was a natural time to seek rest but sometimes you have to take advantage of the opportunity. The next morning, for his part "Fighting Joe" Hooker took Lookout Mountain on the southern flank, in what is called *the battle above the clouds* since the peak of the hill was obscured by clouds. On 25 November Sherman again attacked against Bragg's north flank, but Bragg sent reserves so the attack was contained. But now the idea was: if Hooker could continue to cut into the southern flank Bragg would be forced to weaken the center which Thomas thus could attack. In fact, it was played out in reverse order: the center was attacked after which Hooker could take the flank.

Coordination wasn't total, Grant didn't know exactly what happened – they didn't have radio at the time, and detailed strikers could get lost or get killed in the general commotion. In any case, Grant sent an order with such a striker to Thomas, with the instruction to take and clear out the red force gun pits at the base of Missionary Ridge. When the order reached the brigade in question it became a general signal of attack, the hill was charged *en masse*, the soldiers steadily advancing up the hill – and soon the whole height had been taken. This was considered an impossible feat at the time, frontal assault against a consolidated position was nothing you looked easily upon. The current brigade is even said to have been criticized afterward, no orders had been given to take the hill... This was, of course, wayward formalism since *nothing beats a tactical victory.*

With this gain up the sleeve Hooker could approach the southern flank quite easily, Bragg must give up his positions and was soon in full retreat, and Grant chased after him but let it slide after a few days. The grandiose double envelopment might have failed—it was just about attacks in the middle and the south after which Bragg slipped out of the trap—but nonetheless, Chattanooga was a great Union victory. Grant only lost one-tenth of his 60,000 while Bragg lost 8,000 of which 3,000 prisoners, out of a total of 33,000. In addition, he lost 40 cannons which was not insignificant.

This victory made possible a continued advance towards the vital parts of the South, towards Atlanta, Georgia, and Savannah-by-the-Sea. By this, another large piece would be cut away from the Confederation; with the fall of Vicksburg were lost Texas, Louisiana, and Arkansas, and with the new operation Mississippi, Alabama, Florida and half of Georgia would be lost, only leaving the Carolina States and Virginia. In addition to the conquest of the territory and the plaguing of the home front this maneuver, with an army operating in Lee's back, would prevent him from concentrating all his efforts towards the "northern Virginia theater of operations"; Grant knew that Union attacks up there in the North were difficult, *inter alia* because of the *lack of room for maneuver* we mentioned earlier.

Thus, if the enemy was threatened in the back and the front at the same time an attack in northern Virginia would be easier: the enemy must wage a two-front war, always a difficult art, and for the Confederates with their scarce resources a nightmare. The attack on Atlanta was launched by Sherman in the spring of 1864, Sherman at this point having replaced Grant as G-i-C in the West while Grant was sent to Washington to become G-i-C of all the Union's forces. Strangely enough, there was still the former G-in-C Halleck as a top man; "Chief of Staff" was his title even if nobody really knew what his job was. It was Grant who was in charge, Grant being what Lincoln had searched for long and finally found, a loyal general who fought with what he had and won victories. Grant was given a free hand to formulate his strategy, and in this respect, he realized that the main objective was to crush Lee's army, *the Army of Northern Virginia*. The main effort of the attacks would be in the East, in the region between Richmond and Washington, even if at the same time, Sherman would exert pressure from the West. This was a truly coordinated strategy, a continental strategy, the Union having thus far mostly stumbled around in the dark. It had no strategy at all, having only "on to Richmond" as the slogan and nothing more.

Grant arrived in Washington one day in the spring of 1864. He made little fanfare; when checking in at his hotel the bellman didn't recognize him – and this was remarkable, this was after all the most famous Union general, old *Unconditional Surrender,* the victor of Vicksburg and Chattanooga. And his picture would have been in the news, either as photo or xylograph. But apart from that, the clerk not recognizing him was not so strange for Grant didn't have much of charisma, he aroused no cheer among his personnel for example. Some perhaps noted *the old man* where he passed in the camp but otherwise it was hardly anyone who knew him – primarily, there were no screams, songs, and poems to his honor as it was around McClellan. For his part, Mac, with all his posturing, nevertheless was a soldier's general, he could sit down at the camp fire and share a cigar with the common man. Grant never seems to have done something like this.

Grant came to Washington. The shock at Shiloh had long since had its effect, it was total war and large battles looming. Perhaps the public had realized this too. It was goodbye to the faith in a *coup de main* which would put an end to the war, and a goodbye to voluntary recruitment—for, general conscription was now introduced in the Union and this was extremely unpopular, indeed, even absurd for some—for if propaganda said that they fought for freedom, then why having people forced to fight? There were even riots against the Conscription Law of 1863, protest against this coercive act, a little-known fact. But the law remained in force, the Union army was growing in strength and in the spring of 1864 Grant could launch an attack against Lee from the north while Sherman approached from the south.

Grant had 120,000 men and thought that this was going to be a rather fast affair, done by the summer. But in this, he was deceived. The terrain was wooded and obstructive and any attempt to circumvent Lee's southern flank was prevented by him with this and that counter-measure. "The defense is always stronger than the attack," it says in the proverbial Book of Tactics, and this was now demonstrated, Lee performing a defensive action helped by the lack of room for maneuver in the northern Virginian terrain. Grant had to launch costly frontal attacks but he certainly had reinforcements to cover for his losses. The spring saw a series of battles costing much blood, battles uninteresting from a tactical point of view, being just a series of monotonous blows, like *the Wilderness* and *Spottsylvania* in May. The latter was a victory for the North but a costly one, an "ordinary victory" nevertheless giving Grant new hope for the future: "I am confident the enemy is very shaky."

More bloody battles were fought. For instance, the Union had rather high losses (12,000) at Cold Harbor but no outcry arose in the public opinion because of this, people were rather used to such figures by now. The equally high losses of Burnside at Fredericksburg 1863 belonged to another era. Additionally, Cold Harbor was part of a broader strategy than Fredericksburg had been, it was part of the plan to finally defeat the Confederacy; a strong will lay behind the war effort by this time and the name of that will was Ulysses S. Grant. Now it was the era of "Battle Hymn of the Republic," it was now a perceived crusade – and the European public opinion was no longer for the Confederacy, this view had gone out of style after Gettysburg. Now the opinion idolized the Union which fought for the abolition of slavery, that was the official, propagandistic war goal after Lincoln's Emancipation Declaration on 1 January 1863.

In his operations, Grant constantly tried to circumvent Lee's southern flank, all to be able to attack Richmond and bring the war to a close. But Lee offset the shocks and the front line was extended into something like "a WW1 front," a long, well-fortified siege line running from Richmond to the city of St. Petersburg in the south. This line now saw a stationary war being fought for nine months.

The Confederacy, for its part, launched a cavalry raid in July 1864 up the Virginia valley with Washington as a target. The unit strength was 10,000 and it shook things up in the North for a while but basically, it was harmless. It wasn't the same threat as a similar raid in 1862 when Lee sent Stonewall Jackson up the valley to weaken McClellan's attack on Richmond – and this did indeed become the case then, forces were taken from Mac to reinforce Washington. Now, in 1864, Grant sent two army corps to protect Washington but this changed nothing in the basic strategy, he could remain with the main army before Richmond-Petersburg.

In the spring of 1865, Lee's army was completely starved. It was forced to give up Richmond, the capital that President Davis had wanted to hold on to for as long as possible. Lee cast off with the remains of his army and went west, in the vain hope to join with Joseph Johnston in North Carolina, a force, for its part, being chased by Sherman who now had marched through the vital Confederate states since 1864, pillaging where it went forth. However, Lee's units were defeated one after one, he never reached Johnston, and finally, Lee asked for standstill negotiations with Grant. These took place on 9 April in *Appomattox Court House* and thus the war was virtually over. The Confederacy surrendered rather unconditionally. One detail that Grant could offer was that the officers would be able to keep their swords which was appreciated; the same offer, by the way, was received by the German General Paulus at Stalingrad, like *a spoonful of sugar helping the medicine go down*. Grant also allowed soldiers riding their own horses to keep them and use them in farming.

These *basic* military concessions Grant was authorized to give. Politically, however, the future of the Confederacy was in the hands of the President and Congress.

The meeting itself was spectacular: as usual, Grant had a slightly unkempt demeanor, like a dirty uniform, while Lee was wearing his best uniform with a silken sash. However, this was no joyous occasion for Lee, on the contrary, "I would rather die a thousand deaths than go see General Grant," he said at the time. But Grant received him politely and started chatting about the Mexican War both had participated in. They spoke so long about this that Lee finally had to remind his colleague of the current issue…

After the war, Grant, to begin with, was Army Chief of Staff, and then he became the presidential candidate for the Republicans in the elections of 1868. He did indeed win this election but as president he was unsuccessful. There was corruption among the employees and Grant didn't seem to be able to curb this. In politics, you can't just give orders; instead, it's *the art of the possible* where different means of pressure and maneuvers must be applied, "whip and carrot" etc. The regime's strongman seems to have been Secretary of State Hamilton Fish. Grant lasted two terms as president, a total from 1868 to 1876; he died in 1885.

All things considered, Grant was probably the greatest general of the Civil War. He had a grip of *strategy,* to the war effort *as a whole:* in this matter, he became something of a holist, uniting all the war operations and war zones into one, single expression. People like McClellan and Lee couldn't conceptually connect the western theater of war to the eastern; they saw only the latter, seeing only the dimension Richmond-Washington, having only a march against the enemy capital city on their minds: this and only this should determine the war, they seem to have thought.

Of Grant, it is said that he wasn't a great tactician such as Lee or Jackson. However, for a top general, this isn't required, it is enough to say to your subordinates to fight, it is for them to choose the tactics; the top general, for his part, should focus on strategy. Additionally, in the final stage of the war, there was no room for tactical artistry, the current terrain in Virginia didn't favor maneuvers; instead, the sledgehammer must win the war – and this hammer Grant wasn't afraid to swing. He was a stubborn fellow, he had *staying power* which he showed at Vicksburg when a southern woman teased him and said when he expected to take the fortress. "I don't know," Grant said, "but I will stay here for 20 years if necessary!"

One large, priceless advantage that Grant had in his generalship was *that served himself up.* He started as regimental commander, continued to lead a brigade and then came up on the top level. He had some leeway to make mistakes and learn from them. On the other hand, people like Sherman and McClellan were thrown onto the army level immediately, having virtually no room for making mistakes. This should be remembered when eulogizing Grant.

4. THOMAS "STONEWALL" JACKSON (1824-1863)

THOMAS "STONEWALL" JACKSON WAS BORN in 1824 in Clarksburg, Virginia. The years 1842-46 were spent at West Point and then he became a second lieutenant of artillery. As such, he participated in the Mexican War; at Vera Cruz, he is said to have directed a cannon so well that the whole city was taken thanks to this.

Before the Civil War, Jackson was a teacher at the *Virginia Military Institute* in Lexington, Virginia, a private, state-supported military college. After the outbreak of the war, he chose the Confederate side and participated as a brigade commander at *Bull Run,* the first battle of the war. It was here that he got his nickname; during a critical phase, an officer saw how Jackson stood firm and cried to his men: "Look, there is General Jackson like a stone wall! Rally around the Virginians!" The outcry was heard, the units gathered in the implied direction and the Confederates soon won the battle.

In November 1861 Jackson was promoted Major General and given the command in the Virginia Valley, also called the Shenandoah Valley after the river flowing here: *Oh, Shenandoah, I long to hear you, roll away, you rolling river...*

This was friendly, "blue force" territory, Confederate ground that could serve as a back-door route in an advance toward Washington, in a, from the Confederates' perspective, circumventing operation on the left flank. In the summer of 1862, Jackson launched a legendary campaign in this region and defeated several Union armies: mobility, surprise, and concentration were the watchwords. Jackson was something of a military genius so he deserves the honor of these victories, but as mentioned the valley was blue force territory and the generals he was set against often had their positions thanks to political contacts, not competence.

Before Chancellorsville, the battle where he fell, Jackson particularly took part in the Seven Days battle. Here was not in time at a crucial moment, probably due to the hard-core idea of not fighting on Sundays. This is religious piety gone wrong; for instance, if operations demand it even Jeanne d'Arc thought it right to fight on Sundays. Many a good general have certainly had their bad day, like MacArthur on the first day of the Philippine battle 1941, Montgomery at Arnhem and Bradley during the Ardennnes, so Jackson shouldn't be reduced to nothing for this lapse. After the Seven Days battle, Jackson took part in Second Bull Run in August 1862, Antietam and Fredericksburg in December. At the latter, he had advanced to Lieutenant General, three-star general. He was by this time probably the best of the subordinate Confederate generals, Robert E. Lee's right-hand man – but unfortunately for the Confederation, he fell in the spring of 1863.

Jackson died of blue force fire, *friendly fire* – at the battle of Chancellorsville, on his way back to his own lines after a reconnaissance ride. After the fatal shot, he was taken to a house where he lingered for a week, soaring between life and death, deliriously ranting; you could hear how he gave orders to his division managers as if he was in the thick of battle. But then he calmed down and spoke as the last word, as a spur of the moment, "Let us cross over the river and rest under the shade of the trees." He had indeed *passed over,* crossed the border to the Beyond.

An illumination of Stonewall Jackson's character can be done with this anecdote. A Confederate officer had participated in a battle against some Yankees, of which the latter all had been killed. The Southerner told Jackson this regrettably, he said that it was a shame to have to see such men of valor fall. "But *I* don't want them to live,"

Jackson said, "Kill them all!" Jackson had a strange, absent look in his eyes, like a Biblical prophet. There was something archaic over him, *something completely out of Plutarch,* as someone said of Napoleon. His commander Robert E. Lee was rather easier to fathom, a more transparent personality so to speak.

5. GEORGE B. MCCLELLAN (1826-1885)

HE WAS THE WONDER-CHILD GRADUATING from West Point already as a 19-year-old, having served with distinction in the Mexican War, having constructed a cavalry saddle and having been an observer in the Crimean War – and, on the civil side, having been railway director, a top job in the old-school trade and industry. After the first Bull Run he was appointed Union army commander, in this role creating an orderly and well-equipped army which would advance toward Richmond according to all the rules of the book and which would have the South capitulate by its sheer presence; with a mass army next door, the Confederates would be made to understand that their cause was lost and ask for mercy, peace would be entered and the Union be re-established. The general himself would be lauded as the victor with a capital V and be elected the next US president, the man who in this way quelled the uprising without much blood spilled. Maybe this was his train of thought, and his name was in all events *George Brinton McClellan*.

McClellan became the Union army chief after first Bull Run; he entered in office in the autumn of 1861. Mac replaced General Winfield Scott on this post, a man having received his officer's commission already from Thomas Jefferson in 1808, having participated in the War of 1812 and having been army commander in the Mexican War. Called *Old Guts and Glory* he was a legend, with time a fairly portly type unable to sit a horse, having in his office a specially constructed sofa to sit in; chairs, he couldn't use. This aside, he had an inkling of the immense perspective of defeating the Confederacy: he knew that this was going to be a long war, that it would require hundreds of thousands of men to defeat the Confederates and that the strategy was to strangle and cut up the enemy territory, the embryo to the strategy U. S. Grant would later apply. It wouldn't do with a simple offensive against Richmond – that which almost all, including McClellan, seem to have thought.

McClellan was an eastbound strategist, he gave little for campaigns at the same time being carried out in Tennessee and Kentucky. No, *on to Richmond* was the watchword and Mac suggested that he had the recipe for victory. He had some small gains up the sleeve, fought in West Virginia in the summer, and now he elaborated upon them into epic format. To his soldiers, he had held speeches with Napoleonic rhetoric: "You have won great victories, you have done the impossible..." Napoleon was his idol and he used to pose with his hand tucked into the coat opening like him. Otherwise, Mac made a rather dashing impression with dark hair and a mustache, he sat a horse well and was fairly liked by the common ranker; these were not unimportant features of the man.

McClellan would lead the Union operations and for this was primarily needed a real *army*. In this he had to begin virtually from scratch for the regular army was by then occupied with its usual police activities in the West. True, there were volunteers to fill the ranks and the officer positions but the main problem was spelled *professionalism;* no one thought that the war would last long, all imagining that everything would be resolved with a death blow to Richmond after which all could go home and celebrate. Instead, you needed an army that could sustain a modicum of defeat, an elastic unit with *staying power* which could operate against a well organized, skilled enemy – and indeed, it was recognized that the Confederates had better quality of both soldiers and officers, having many farmland guys used to riding and having received the majority of trained officers with the formation of the Confederation in 1861. Nonetheless, Mac managed to complete his work, he launched *the Army of the Potomac* as a strong, well-equipped force, one which hopefully wouldn't run from the Confederates as the first unit had done at Bull Run in July 1861. Lincoln, for his part, insisted that the army would march toward Richmond as quickly as possible but McClellan knew better. Another defeat would be disastrous, now it was about operating meticulously under the watchword "better safe than sorry".

So, it was only in the spring of 1862 that McClellan marched, having a clever plan to go by, an *indirect strategy* in which Richmond wouldn't be attacked straight on but from the south with an amphibious, circumventive motion. It was the *campaign on the Peninsula,* where the York Peninsula became a theater of war after maritime transport and landing of the Union army. Lee, however, parried this shock and went to the offensive – but McClellan kept his composure and retreated with his forces in cohesion. That was *the Battle of the Seven Days.* After this, however, Lincoln lost patience with his general, Mac in their dealings often being haughty and secretive. And he hadn't delivered the promised victory.

Lincoln, therefore, dismissed McClellan in August, only to reinstate him in September after general Pope failed in the Second Battle of Bull Run. Now the initiative was with the Confederacy; Lee launched an invasion of Maryland and hoped to win this state for the Confederacy but it all came to grief, McClellan in no uncertain terms opposing him at Antietam. This was a bloody battle, tactically undecided, but Lee retreated and ditched the invasion plan, thus the whole affair was a strategic victory for the Union. However, Lincoln wanted Mac to pursue but Mac saw himself unable to do this—so he got fired, for the second and last time—and now Mac went into politics, becoming the presidential candidate for the Democrats in 1864. Lincoln wasn't amused but what could he do. He even won the election himself in the end. As for the politics of the war, what concerned Lincoln was that the Democrats, if they came to power, seemed to favor an end of the war with a compromise, and Lincoln was against any compromise: death or glory, Union or nothing! It was a costly principle but it probably saved America from several subsequent squabbles between North and South, wars which might have appeared from time to time if the Civil War had ended with a compromise in the 1860s.

In his essay on Grant, Bengtsson paints McClellan as something close to a clown, almost a clinical idiot. True, Mac had a histrionic strain to him, almost like "the other Mac," Douglas MacArthur of the 20th century; like him, he played the role of himself. But he was no fool. We would personally put Mac in the "near great" category as a general – for he never won any clear-cut victory, and winning battles is indeed what generals are expected to do, as Montgomery of Alamein said. But in *the Army of the Potomac* which Mac created the professionalism was implicit and this was important, he forged it into an instrument that continued to operate even when led by less skilled generals than himself, this army which became the backbone of the whole Union army. It held its ground at Gettysburg and was the main strength in the offensive of 1864-65. Then you cannot, of course, deny Mac's other shortcomings: he was arrogant against his top commander Lincoln, he showed his contempt for this military amateur a bit too much, for example by coming up with objections to given orders. However, at the top level, some discussion must be allowed to occur. A general is a soldier but not a private soldier having to say, "ay-ay sir" to everything. But Mac seems to have taken it too far, he never bit the bullet; instead, he was always complaining about things like the weather and not having enough equipment.

6. GEORGE A. CUSTER (1839-1876)

WHEN THE AMERICANS HAD WON the Revolutionary War in 1783 they simply disbanded the army. A standing army in peacetime they wouldn't have—for this was the New World, the promised land, not subject to the laws of necessity governing the Old World—the Old World with its despotism, its repression, and its standing armies.

Freedom would prevail in the New World, it was agreed. So, the army was dissolved, a loose federation was formed and everyone went home for business as usual; the thirteen colonies were like thirteen states, almost like sovereign countries all of them. However, soon it was discovered that anarchy loomed on the horizon. There was little law and order, trade didn't work properly, there wasn't a common currency and the territory was threatened by Brits in the North and American Indians in the West – so they had to write a new constitution, replacing the 1777 *Articles of Confederation* with the 1789 *Constitution for the United States of America*. They had to balance the divine principle of *freedom* with the less rosy but essential principle of *order*.

For the sake of national defense, the 1789 Constitution stated that a standing army would be established. For the desired *more perfect union* of the thirteen colonies that the Constitution was talking about, an army of this kind was required for "the common defense". It was impossible to rely on amateurs and voluntary action when it came to guarding the borders against the British in the North, the French in the Louisiana area in the West, the Spanish in Florida in the South, and to prevent Indians from terrorizing settlers. The army ranks were to be made up of professional soldiers, full-time employed private soldiers who signed on for a couple of years at a time. But there were *officers* also, and by this time the need for real *officer training* arose; France already had its École Militaire which Napoleon attended, a school then moving to Saint-Cyr where it has remained ever since. Further, in the UK was the war academy Sandhurst and now the United States would follow these examples, leading to the creation of the war academy of *West Point* in 1802. This was a fortress on the Hudson River that Benedict Arnold had failed to deliver to the British during the Revolutionary War. On a distinctive rock, the facilities sat, a central outlook point which dominated the river and the lowland. The crest or plateau is called *the plain* and on this was erected some brick buildings to house the new college.

In the early days, West Point was primarily a school of artillery and engineering. These service branches required a great deal of formal education while the infantry and cavalry mostly demanded sense and sensibility and a feel for the situation. Artillery and engineering were the top branches of the old-school army, the most status filled career ways – and to qualify in these you needed to be good at mathematics and geometry, two subjects riding high on the West Point curriculum. Furthermore, there were classes in English, French, tactics, history and natural sciences. Concerning the natural sciences, hereby an anecdote of a student being flunked after this examination dialogue: "Please elaborate on the element of silicon." "I will elaborate on the element of silicon. Silicon is a gas." "Thank you, that'll be enough!", the teacher said. The student was James McNeill Whistler (1834-1903), the painter to be.

But the cadets weren't always in the classroom. Some basic soldier training was also included. However, there weren't any specific, tangible courses in the art of leading military units. This would be handled later, in the real world, when the cadet was posted in a field unit. An important part of the historic West Point was to learn the trainee *drill and discipline;* for the latter, there was a system where you started the four-year course with 200 points and for different offenses, points were subtracted, called *demerits* or remarks. One that took a record number of demerits was a certain *George Armstrong Custer*; he finished last in his class in this regard and he did it on purpose; "rather notorious than unknown," as we say in Sweden (*"hellre okänd än okänd"*).

G. A. Custer was born in Ohio in 1839. His family came originally from Germany; his grandfather's grandfather is said to have been called Paul Kuester. In the summer of 1857 Custer arrived at West Point after going with steamboat from New York, sailing up the Hudson River which the fortress overviews from its rock. As for his school days, the whole course was five years in his days, not four as is otherwise the standard before and since – but this novelty had no effect since the course for the class of 1857 was prematurely terminated in the spring of 1861 because of the Civil War. This was when the circa ten southern states had seceded and Fort Sumter had been attacked in April; this was the final impulse for Lincoln had already branded secession as rebellion, having enrolled volunteers to suppress the whole affair.

Four years is the norm for the West Point course, even that rather much; however, this has got to do with the educational system at large. The British Sandhurst and Swedish Karlberg courses have traditionally only been two years, presuming that the cadet already has basic nine-year education plus secondary education of two to four years. My impression is that in the US, the cadet can go directly to West Point after high school, having then ten years of basic education behind him.

Custer graduated from West Point in the spring of 1861. He went to New York for a few days of leave and then on to Washington. After having bought a horse and having received his orders at the Ministry of War he went directly to McDowell's army which was in the field just outside the capital city. There, in northern Virginia on the south side of the Potomac River, a battle was fought at the beginning of June which was a defeat for the Union: *the First Battle of Bull Run*. Both sides were rather disorganized and it was difficult to tell friend from foe, but the Confederation under Joseph E.

Johnston in due course received reserves making the scales tip; the Union forces decided to fall back, a movement soon developing into a disorderly escape, leaving the cavalry to protect the rear, which Custer as an officer of the cavalry just did. Reportedly, he was one of the last Union officers to leave the battlefield.

Custer served during the whole war as a Union officer of cavalry. In this age of more efficient small-caliber gunfire, the role of the cavalry was mainly reduced to tasks like reconnaissance and advance and rearguard action. And, sometimes, more-or-less substantial cavalry raids. Personally, Custer cut a dashing figure in his long, curly blond hair, Nietzsche style mustache and black silk uniform, having something of the "English Civil War" cavalier about him. However, not everyone was impressed by him as this anecdote tells.

It was in the spring of 1865, Custer as Brigadier General serving in the *corps de chasse* chasing the remnants of Lee's army. In one instance, Custer was close to one of Lee's corps commanders, James Longstreet, to whom he said:

"If you don't surrender, I will have to demonstrate against you."

"Demonstrate as much as you wish," Longstreet said.

After the cessation of hostilities, the Union army officer cadre was cut down and Custer was demoted to Lieutenant Colonel, this being the price to remain in the reduced army. In 1866, he was given operational responsibility for the *7th Cavalry Regiment* in Kansas, and now followed five years of war against the prairie Indians, two years of stationing in Kentucky and finally, in 1873, deployment in the North-West. In this area, parts of the 7th Cavalry would perish at *Little Bighorn.*

US Army had the role of enforcing the law in the West, representing the authority of the state. "The Law West of the Pecos" wasn't Roy Bean, it was the army. It would keep track of the Indians who sometimes attacked settlers; cavalry patrols were good for this, as strong points having the famous western forts. For its part, 7th

Cavalry had the heraldic colors of yellow and black, later, during the Vietnam War, taken up by the helicopter-borne *AirCav* which traced its ancestry back to Custer's regiment.

As for the run-up to Little Bighorn, the government of the United States in the 1870s had declared war against the Sioux since they hadn't given up *the Black Hills*. This was an area in the North-West, in Dakota territory which the Indians first had been promised to keep. But when gold was found in the region the government broke its promise. The 7th Cavalry had been deployed to the Dakota territory in 1873. In June 1876, it was sent out on reconnaissance after the Sioux and their allies, a large gathering of rampaging Indians, and commander of one of the patrolling forces was Custer. On June 25, he got to see a large Native American village at the Little Bighorn river and he chose to attack immediately without the support of the other detachments deployed in the vicinity.

It was one of the Indian scouts of the Custer unit having gotten sight of the camp; reportedly, no white man of the unit could see it. Custer, for the day wearing a hat of badger skin, calfskin leather trousers and leather jacket with fringes, chose to believe the Indians. So he decided to attack. Why he took this decision we will never know because he and his men died in battle—but—it is believed that he wanted to have the honor of a great victory, a victory that was only his. And then, to politically use such a victory to aim for Congress, the Senate, the White House...?

Custer wanted the whole honor for himself. He even partitioned his detachment further by sending an officer by name Benteen to scout along a river valley, in a completely different direction. He seems to have disliked Benteen and wanted to have him out of the way when cutting his laurels. For the attack proper, Custer concocted a rather clever plan including bypass and flank attack, combined with the binding of a perceived front. Three squadrons (cavalry companies) under one Major Reno would go south of the Little Bighorn river and attack the Indian camp in full view of it, thus binding the front, while Custer with the main force—five squadrons—would go north of the river behind some hills to attack the enemy in the flank. In theory, this was a sound plan but it faltered because of the Indians being so numerous, and that the Custer part of the approach was detected at an early stage. Custer for his part is said to have underestimated the enemy, he never thought that Indians would be able to defeat US Army in a pitched battle, which until then, of course, had not happened. As for critique, you might say that Custer was over-confident, forgetting this: *never expect the enemy to behave as you expect him to do.*

Indeed, Custer's plan was sound: to bind the enemy in the front, and circumvent his flank in the protection of a few hills. But he underestimated the enemy and overestimated himself.

With Benteen out of the way the approach began. Major Reno's three squadrons crossed the river and came in sight of the Indian camp at the same time as the Custer's force continued north of the river, hidden by the hills. Regarding Reno's men, they soon met fierce resistance by mounted Indians coming at them, soon having the troopers surrounded. The Indians were armed with rifles as were the troopers (the latter with the breech-loaded Winchester 1873). Reno's unit suffered great losses so he decided to pull back and retreat over the river, heading for the hills Custer had just passed. With a few men, Reno entrenched himself and held out until Benteen arrived on the site a few days later to rescue them.

In other words, Reno had failed to bind the enemy in the front. In any case, Custer continued his progress. Come to the end of the line of hills he was surprised by mounted Indians *en masse* on his left flank: via a pass in the line of hills Indian horsemen rushed forth and hit the Custer column like a fist, whereby the column was cut up and became a few small isolated strong points. The intended surprise had been completely lost; indeed, Custer himself had been taken by surprise by the Indians. These had taken the initiative and now attacked the dismounted troopers with rifles and arrows, circling around the different strong points and subduing them one by one.

Despite the army having good firearms—Colt revolvers and Winchester rifles—they couldn't fully avert the attacks; the mounted Indians came closer and closer and finally dismounted, in the end killing the soldiers in a melee with tomahawks. They went forth with the battle cry of, *"hokahey"* (a good day to die). A true warrior says this both of himself and his enemies; the true warrior goes into battle ready to die.

All men of the current, "bypass" cavalry force died, including Custer, having his famous *last stand* among his men. The total death toll of the eight squadrons present, Reno's three and Custer's five, was 265 dead and 52 injured.

After the battle the Indians left the place; the Sioux chief Crazy Horse went east and the seer Sitting Bull westward. For his part, Crazy Horse was later defeated and had to surrender while Sitting Bull was defeated twice and then retreating through the snow and cold to Canada with his remaining companions. After the battle of Greasy Grass five years later he also gave in, having reached the limits of its powers. This was the final political act of the Indian cause, the last move of the Indians as an independent force. The Black Hills were subsequently taken from the Indians and made into a mining area.

The Battle of Little Bighorn may have been a very small business compared with many Civil War battles. But it deserves its place as a historic battle for several reasons: it was one of the few, perhaps the *only* time the Indians defeated whites in a pitched battle. Furthermore, it was not only operationally but in reality a *Vernichtungsschlacht*, a battle where one side is completely wiped out as a fighting force. The mythical dimension of such a debacle must be apprehended by all students of history; Little Bighorn represents the defeat, a defeat with a capital D. It's an American Waterloo. That said, it must of course also be remembered that this victory didn't lead to any political gains for the Indians, it rather marked the end of the Indian independence. Not long after this Indian tribes stopped being regarded as contracting parties and the Indians collectively became US citizens instead.

Little Bighorn was truly mythical, taking place in sublime terrain. These Dakota plains are magnificently desolate, from the Montana Hill where Custer fell you can see for miles. It is archaic land, as the nearby Black Hills with its shamanistic meaning to the Indians, these mountains of dark forests, ravines and slopes, barely passable in the normal way. It was a landscape loaded with meanings and symbols for the Indians' dreams, Wert says in his Custer biography; it was a dreamland bordering on our world.

An archaic land indeed. In Dakota, we also find *Mount Rushmore* with its four presidents carved out of the rock, Washington, Jefferson, Lincoln, and Teddy Roosevelt. Europe has no similar monument with ancient-monumental feeling, we must go to southern China's colossal Buddhas or Egypt's Abu Simbel to find something in the same class. Finally, it's in the Dakota region many *dinosaur skeletons* have been found. The antediluvian giant lizards we see in museums all over the world often come from *the Dakota Badlands,* the hilly stone desert which is one of a kind.

7. JOHN J. PERSHING (1861-1948)

IN THE SPRING OF 1917, PRESIDENT Wilson declared war on Germany. The short-term reason was that Germany had started *unrestricted submarine warfare*, thereby also threatening American shipping. The United States was thus engaged in WWI on the side of the so-called Entente, England, France, Italy, and Russia, opposing the Central Powers which were Germany and Austria. For the US, this was the era of general conscription and "Uncle Sam wants you for the US Army". And the head of *the American Expeditionary Force* was *John Joseph Pershing*.

Pershing had recently commanded a certain punitive expedition to Mexico. He was presented to the government as one of several candidates. And when they saw him they directly chose him; tall, well groomed and a soldier through and through. As intimated he had just led a small army in the field in the hunt for Pancho Villa, fair enough, but how would he manage to lead a more formidable army against a well-entrenched, well-equipped opponent as the Kaiser's Germany? Pershing had a huge amount of work to create an American army which was good enough to be inserted into this total war. Like McClellan in 1861, he had to fight amateurism. More about the technical and tactical details later.

When the United States had declared war on Germany, France and England demanded that the US would send some troops as quickly as possible; only a small contingent would do much to morale, it was said, it would have a symbolically important role. The Allies had lost one million only during the battles of the past year, and indeed there were cries of joy as the American soldiers marched down Champs Elysées *au chapeaux de cow-boy*, the field hat dating from the Civil War, the only difference being that now it was in khaki, then it was black. In addition, the American soldiers had khaki uniforms and helmets of the English type.

Apart from the white-bearded Uncle Sam in the poster, Pershing became the symbol of the American Expeditionary Force (AEF). Now—apart from "fighting the Hun"—he launched a sustained campaign to keep the force gathered, a political ambition to have all the American units under US command which perhaps was natural in this context. Haig and Foch, for their part, wanted to have the reinforcements send hither and thither, they wanted to have holes plugged and the American troops seemed good for this. But Pershing refused. However, as Ludendorff launched his surprise offensives in the spring of 1918 Pershing gave in, *tout ce que nous avons est à vous,* he said, for indeed he knew French. American divisions and brigades were sent left, right and center to reinforce any threatened front sector, for now, it was a struggle for life. Next, in August, when the German storm wave had been contained the Americans could have their own front sector, *Meuse-Argonne* in the middle of the Western Front. They could soon attack as a unified, American army and as such, it fought until the war ended in November.

The American arrival in WWI was of symbolic importance. The French and the British were exhausted at the time and needed new blood. Then you can argue exactly how much the Americans contributed in the number of men and guns and so on, and you can emphasize that most of their equipment was French or English made; the self-produced American items hadn't noticeably begun to arrive at the units at the time of the front operations proper. But as intimated, the American insertion was in a way decisive, it was the tipping of the scales. It gave back *the fighting spirit* to the exhausted British and French.

During the build-up phase, Pershing worried if his unit would stand the trial, stand the test of combat. Would his officers and rankers, used to hunt Indians and Mexican bandits, face up to the requirements of total war? And how would all the new recruits take it, all the freshly recruited national service soldiers? The regular army could only set up four divisions, this wouldn't last long in a war against Germany – instead, now the estimated need was for *100* American divisions. Thus, national service = conscription was required. The war that they would fight differed significantly from the wars Americans recently had experienced, the requirements were infinitely higher now. An example of the naïve spirit was when Theodore Roosevelt, the ex-president having been a cavalry officer in the war in Cuba, offered to set up a volunteer regiment. Wilson said, "thanks but no thanks" and he was right in doing so, this was no place for happy amateurs. The army to be sent overseas must be a professional force, it would end up in a battle environment requiring martinet style discipline in order not to break up by the first artillery salvo.

Which brings us to the operational nature of WWI. I previously showed how in the Civil War the defense had become stronger than the attack, it being harder to attack a position of reasonably long-range rifles than a position of smooth-bore muskets. Now the defense had grown even more in strength with bolt-action rifles and machine guns, the former with approximately 1,000 meter range of fire, as well as with the method of sending reinforcements to threatened sectors by railway. As for the artillery, it had developed remarkably. While it was true that even an attacker now could make use of the new back-load, long-range pieces, on the Western Front where there was little room for maneuvering, the accumulation of pieces tended to strengthen the defense. Regarding pieces with shorter ranges of fire these met difficulties when grouping on the battlefield since the cannon service became easy targets for small caliber fire (range of fire 1,000 meters).

As for "room for maneuvering" this might need to be clarified. The Western Front terrain at large was characterized by open terrain, wide fields well suited for mobile operations, but with four national armies crammed into this region the *strategic* room for maneuver was reduced. The *tactical* room for maneuver was reduced by artillery fire plowing up the landscape, destroying drainage and creating a sea of mud. It should, however, be added that the artillery, correctly inserted, was important for all kinds of operations; even if the defender, for example, could take protection during the firestorm, well-directed artillery fire could also prevent the timely delivery of the defender's reinforcements.

Regarding reinforcements, they could strategically be brought forward by rail. In the Battle of the Marne in 1914 the French used taxis for this, and later, at Verdun, trucks in large scale. All of this was an example of the *mechanization of the defense,* and with the arrival of the tank, the offense was also mechanized. The crucial role of the tank, however, was only to be seen in the WWII.

After the war, Pershing became *Army Chief of Staff,* the highest military position. A contentious issue was the future of general conscription; Wilson had introduced it in connection with the outbreak of the war and Pershing now wanted to keep it, in a conventional reaction of the bureaucrat: faced with a reduced organization he always says no. But Pershing had to give in, Congress decided on a return to the professional army as was the model before the war. Rankers and officers would be ordinary employees and the overall unit strength would be about 100,000 men with the National Guard as a reserve. Generals like Marshall and Patton reverted to their pre-war ranks. In their generation, only MacArthur managed to remain on the general level.

Having left the office of army chief Pershing got promoted to *General of the Army,* five-star general corresponding to a European field marshal. He retired and could see WWII from the ringside. His old friend Pétain became French head of state, leading the regime cooperating with the Germans, a fact not well liked in the US – but Pershing didn't mind this, to him Pétain was always Pétain, the savior of the French at Verdun. A certain de Gaulle didn't want anything to do with Pétain – but, when de Gaulle was on a visit to the USA in 1944 to secure support for his Free French forces, he at one time met Pershing who said:

"How is Pétain?"

8. GEORGE C. MARSHALL (1880-1959)

YOU COULD SAY: THE COALITION WARS 1790-1815 met the challenge of the French upsurge. And the World Wars 1914-45 met the challenge of the German upsurge. In this pattern, you could say that WWII was a continuation of the power struggle syndrome intimated by WWI. The Pacific War, for its part, was part of the Japanese attempt to dominate China, an ambition held since 1937 and maybe even earlier, since the beginning of the 20th century.

A central American figure in the World War Era was *George Catlett Marshall*. Born in 1880 his career went straight ahead, having an early apex in attending the General Staff school in Fort Leavenworth, Kansas, a breeding ground for future generals. In 1917, he was sent to the Western Front as chief of staff of the US 1st division, *Big Red One*, the first unit sent over. Despite it being an elite unit, much work remained before it would be battle ready. Marshall carried out his work to satisfaction, once even daring to oppose Pershing himself. Pershing had criticized a division commander but Marshall intervened and said that the criticism was unjustified. Pershing duly took note of this staff officer who later became chief of staff for the entire American Expeditionary Force – AEF.

Marshall was close to being appointed General (Brigadier; maybe Major General) at the end of the war but it wasn't to be, he must revert to his pre-war rank of Captain. The inter-war years Marshall spent in relative anonymity, apart from when he was head of the newly created *Infantry School* at Fort Benning, Georgia. Here he introduced a conceptual innovation with *mobile warfare* at the forefront, the so-called "Benning Revolution". Until then the doctrine had been characterized by the Western Front trench war, its "siege tactics" focused on breaking a fortified opponent with massive artillery bombardment and methodical advance, with tactical basics like *surprise* and *bypass* neglected.

Thankfully, Marshall had the ability to see beyond this, to free himself from this standard. For example, in a paper he brought forth the idea that operations often are chaotic; it is one thing to plan troop movements on a map, another to translate them into reality, which strikingly recalls Moltke the Elder's dictum of, "no plan survives the first fifteen minutes of hostile contact". Marshall had the ability to conceptualize war, de-emphasizing then obvious elements like trench lines, position war and war of attrition, instead focusing on the unpredictability of events, mobility and the role of the infantry.

At the end of the 1930s Marshall was deputy army commander and in September 1939 he became *Army Chief of Staff*, i.e. army commander which at the time was the same as top defense chief since army chief was considered as *primus inter pares* in relation to the naval commander, the *Naval Chief of operations*. Marshall didn't believe that he would become the head of the army, precisely because he had been deputy army commander before – for, in the spirit of Moltke, top commands were usually given to more distinct "fighter" types while the staff officer type that Marshall somewhat embodied would be held back, avoiding that the top positions were occupied by figures excelling in planning and peacetime maneuvers.

Bellatores, not *oratores*, were favored at the top spots. However, Marshall proved to be a fine blend of both, leading his land to victory on all fronts in WWII. One of his doctrines in the construction and management of the armed forces was that the army was the main arms branch and that the air force and fleet supported it, stressing the need of substantial ground forces to defeat the enemy. This truism meant Marshall must emphasize this again to President Roosevelt (who could be led astray by the development in the field of military aviation). Roosevelt wanted to give priority to an arm that could be deployed without the political outcry ensuing from an army deployment. But Marshall took him out of that delusion; he more-or-less told him that boots on the ground were necessary to force the enemy out of his foxhole to sign the peace agreement.

After the war, Marshall, in turn, was a mediator in the Chinese Civil War, Secretary of State and Defense Secretary. He served the Truman Democratic administration but was more of an apolitical force, a loyal servant heeding the call when the *Commander-In-Chief* called. Marshall retired in 1951, took off his general *persona* and started to grow roses, silently or not so silently deflecting the critique of the Republican right-wing accusing him of having betrayed China to the Communists, this because of Marshall's failure to mediate in the Chinese Civil War. During his comrade Eisenhower's presidential campaign in 1952, people wanted Ike to make a stand against these McCartyists, putting Ike in a difficult position because he could not disown the McCarty faction completely, and Marshall was a man he had gladly served under. Ike never spoke out against the accusations against Marshall of having contributed in selling out China. But Marshall, for his part, didn't make much of this, he knew that in politics certain rules apply and that personal friendships are in another realm. Marshall said: "You have as much freedom in politics as you have in a prison."

Marshall was a formal, reserved man. Even the children to whom he became a stepfather must call him Mr. Marshall. But he also had an informal strain, like leaving all things military behind him in retirement; he cared more about tending to his roses than commenting on the tenth anniversary of the D-Day. In this, he was different from Ike who, for better or worse, maintained his general persona almost unto his last breath.

9. DOUGLAS MACARTHUR (1880-1964)

LET ME TELL YOU ABOUT *Douglas MacArthur,* a legend among American generals. Many hated him when he was alive and many do so today. Even in my country, Sweden, we find a branch of the MacArthur-hate club—but—let it here be known that *I* am not a member of that club.

The MacArthur family was of Scottish origin. It was part of the clan Campbell and was originally called *MacArtair;* the latter part of the name should be identical with the mythic "Arthur" – King Arthur, the man with the Knights of the Round Table and the Holy Grail. Clan Campbell's motto was *Listen! O listen!* and its colors were green, black and gold.

Douglas' grandfather came to the US as a child in 1815, and he later had a son named Arthur which was 16 years old when the Civil War broke out. He wanted to enlist immediately but his father advised him to first attend a private military school in Illinois. This Arthur did, and in 1862 he was able to enlist in Wisconsin's 24th Infantry Regiment, the so-called *Milwaukee Regiment;* Milwaukee is a city in Wisconsin which is one of the states in the Midwest, which meant that it belonged to the Union. Arthur became an adjutant and soon was promoted for valor; there were no medals for bravery then, only the Purple Heart for wounded and *the Congressional Medal of Honor* given for extraordinary feats. Still today this is the United States' supreme military award, even though I think it's illogical that it's "congressional" – for it should be "presidential" because of the President being Commander in Chief.

Among other things, Arthur MacArthur participated in the Battle of Chattanooga 1863 in the storming of Missionary Ridge, the mythological taking of the height which hadn't strictly been ordered – but Arthur was one of the front-runners, he might even have planted the regimental colors at the top, and this and other deeds gave him the command of the regiment for the rest of the war. It was part of Sherman's Army, on the march to the sea and then north. An anecdote from this time is of the election of 1864, the whole regiment going off to cast its vote, but when it was found that the regimental commander was too young to vote Arthur put down the foot, he said to the election official that if the Colonel can't vote then no one in the regiment can. Cheers from the soldiers and *exeunt omnis.*

Arthur MacArthur's post-war career was not so remarkable, commanding diverse Western forts. For his part, Douglas was born in such a station in 1880. He had two older brothers, one of whom came to serve in the navy during WWI; he died in 1923 and was called Arthur, for in every generation MacArthur there has been an Arthur – and Douglas himself honored this tradition by naming his own son Arthur, which took place in 1938. Arthur the elder's career came to naught; he might have wanted to become army chief but the current Secretary of War Taft was his enemy so he died frustrated, even refusing a military funeral which says a lot of this old war hero, Arthur MacArthur. His hopes were instead transferred to the son.

Douglas indeed eventually reached the level of the army commander, the top military position of the Republic. Prior to that, he had served with distinction in the First World War and been commander of West Point. In the autumn of 1935, he resigned to instead go to the *Philippines* and it was now that the interesting part of Mac's life began. He would become the head of the American military mission in this half-colonial possession. The archipelago was under a governor but it was promised autonomy, effective July 1946, a promise MacArthur was part in fulfilling even if the timetable became a bit tight; the Japanese occupation came in between. MacArthur, for his part, enjoyed life in the Philippines and could socialize on an equal footing with the local elite. However, it has been intimated that MacArthur wasn't on a par with anyone, he was a vain man who played the role of MacArthur wherever he went. While I don't belong to the anti-Mac faction I admit that he was a bit haughty and histrionic in his manners. However, all told, this dramatic strain at crucial points also enabled him to win allies and friends. See William Manchester's *American Caesar* for details; in this bio, we both find criticism of Mac's histrionics and an appreciation of this stylization of his manners.

In 1938 Mac's Philippine term of office ended. But he wanted to stay on the islands and assist it in its defense so he took his leave of the army and became a freelance consultant for the government of the Republic of the Philippines. Their President at the time was called Manuel Quezon. The situation at the time in East Asia was a bit troublesome with an expansionist Japan, the Empire in 1937 having started to conquer all of China, and because of this situation, Roosevelt soon recalled MacArthur into American service. Generals can never completely retire, they can always be recalled into duty this way.

In the year of 1941, MacArthur was responsible for the defense of the Philippines. He had 12,000 US Army servicemen and 110,000 Filipino conscripts, also approximately 20 bombers and 50 fighter aircraft. It was a rather fine force but Washington knew that against a determined attacker it was without prospects; for example, the archipelago was rather large, it was impossible to defend all the possible inroads of an attacker. The war plan was based on the possibility of relieving the islands by sea but this plan came to naught after the attack on Pearl Harbor, the intended escort ships were mostly sunk there. So, Mac was not in an enviable position – and it was aggravated by the fact that he wasn't mentally prepared for the Japanese attack. His actions on the first day of war left a lot to be desired.

It was on 7 December 1941, which was the 8 in the Philippines due to it being located on the east side of the date limit. And the Japanese attacked Pearl Harbor. And at about the same time it harassed the Philippines with air strikes – and because of misunderstanding, all the B-17 aircraft were deployed in the airfields in peacetime fashion, thus becoming fat targets for Japanese air attacks. Half of the bombers and one-third of the fighters were destroyed on the ground. Mac acted lamely this day, he had a notoriously bad day; this even his admirer Manchester admits. Mac, of course, realized that a Japanese attack against Southeast Asia was to be expected, but maybe he suspected that they would bypass the Philippines to avoid a war with the US. However, in a war anything can happen; a commander must not create a mental image, as Napoleon said. You should not assume that the enemy will behave the way you think.

Mac had lost many aircraft and after a while, he had no air force at all; some were shot down and the rest were rebased to Australia, giving the Japanese total air superiority. On 22 December came the invasion of the main island *Luzon*, the Philippines northernmost island with the capital Manila; the Japanese strength was 80,000, twice as much as what Mac had, which is why he immediately retreated to the so-called Bataan peninsula in the Manila region, a well-fortified bastion. The retreat itself went well but otherwise, the situation was dire, the defending force now being besieged without any hope of rescue. As intimated, no fleet could be deployed and sent to the archipelago, the American Pacific fleet being reduced in Pearl Harbor, severely crippled for the time being. To make a long story short, the Bataan force capitulated in May 1942 and the men were led away to prison camps – but the Japanese were unprepared to take care of so many prisoners, they didn't have supplies to all, so the march into captivity caused many deaths and became known as the "Bataan Death March". Disregarding Civil War battles this was the first time an American army surrendered, it was the US Army's biggest defeat ever. For its part, Little Bighorn 1876 was mentioned earlier in this study as an annihilation battle, a *Vernichtungsschlacht*, the whole US force being wiped out – but as noted it was only a regimental detachment of eight companies, not an army proper. Philippines 1942 was a bitter pill to swallow – however, the US at large was undefeated and now a spirit of revenge surged. For instance, when the Doolittle raid had been launched, in the official declaration it was said to be a revenge for Bataan. The atom bomb in 1945 was also perceived thus.

Defeat and disaster, captivity and humiliation – but this was not to be the fate for Mac. He had been ordered by Roosevelt to leave Bataan, leave the Philippines and head off to Australia to start organizing a counter-offensive, ultimately aiming at reclaiming the Philippines and defeating Japan. So, on 11 March Mac packed and left, accompanied by wife, son, and housemaid and boarding a torpedo boat, which by an adventurous nightly ride took them away from the islands and further towards the south. After a change to aircraft, Australia was in due time reached.

To leave your army in this way wasn't exactly heroic. But Mac was *ordered* out, and other commanders having left their armies in the lurch are certainly Napoleon after the Egyptian campaign and Rommel who left North Africa in the late autumn of 1942; they were ordered out without any substantial damage to their reputations. Mac here mostly reminds you of Napoleon: the retreat in question was not heroic but this nadir also meant that from now on, the only way was up. They had their best work ahead of them. Mac was in Australia and now he really was the right man in the right place. For starters, his voice broadcast on the radio had a soothing effect on the public opinion at home in the United States (*I made it out, and I shall return*). Further, he now drew up a bold plan for the next stage of the war against Japan—for, at the time being, everyone in Australia was preparing for a Japanese invasion, the government planning to evacuate the whole northern part and draw the line of defense far in the south of the continent to defend its vital parts —but Mac thought differently, he decided to establish an advance base well north of Australia, on New Guinea's southern coast: *Port Moresby*. Said and done, an airbase was built and troops were sent in, American and Australian, and this and other operations drove the Japanese away towards New Guinea's northern coast. The threat to Australia, imagined or not, was eliminated. With this conceptually and tangibly daring move Mac secured the situation. He laid a ground on which victory could be built.

Mac knew strategy, he was not merely a thespian *prima donna*. Mac's detractors see only the latter part of him, the histrionics and rhetoric, forgetting that he had been a victorious commander in WWI in the furious battle environment of the Western Front. And you don't choose a madman to lead West Point. For his part, Liddell Hart named MacArthur the best American general at the time. In 1942 Mac was 60 and that's no age for a general; his mind was young and he more than enough mastered elements like air support and amphibious warfare. This he showed in the subsequent operations when base after base was taken on New Guinea and neighboring islands, many of them being bypassed, using the almost unlimited room for maneuver the Pacific theater offered. In the South Pacific Mac commanded a combined force of army, navy and air force while US Navy proper had its own offensive going in the Central Pacific, both of these attacks in 1944 pointing at the Philippines. The archipelago could have been bypassed, it was a strategic dead end, but because of it being election year a spectacular victory would help FDR's chances of winning so a full-scale invasion was decided on. It could remind you of 1864 when the fall of Atlanta facilitated the Lincoln election victory that year. Further, what spoke in favor of an invasion was the fact that the US had promised the Philippines independence in 1946 and the fact that Mac had made his "I shall return" statement. In private Roosevelt was no admirer of Mac, on the contrary, but officially the two men's ambitions now coincided so the official agenda was *on to the Philippines.*

In planning the assault a methodical approach was first held forth, like taking the southernmost island of Mindanao first; then, like climbing a ladder, taking island after island and finally reaching the jewel in the crown, Luzon. But when in September it was discovered that the defense of the islands was weak, Admiral Halsey suggested that they would go directly to an island north of Mindanao, Leyte. It would be rather bold to land an army here because the island was situated 800 km beyond the umbrella of aerial support; Mac's air force commander Kenney had always impressed that they must have air support for operations, operating with the aerial support umbrella, and Mac had hitherto followed this advice. But now Mac decided to act on Halsey's inspiration and let the army get support from naval aviation, from carrier-based aircraft, a conceptually unorthodox move.

On 16 October MacArthur set sail with his armada. At midnight, it was in the vicinities of Leyte and it waited for the dawn for the attack to begin. Then the horizon was lit up by the salvos from the large-caliber guns of the battleships, Mac from the ship Nashville watching it all circa 3 km away from Leyte proper. In addition to the island, veiled in clouds of gun smoke, you could see attack aircraft in the sky and landing boats heading for the island. Soon the beach in question was taken and a bridgehead was established, it all being rather similar to the D-day in Normandy. Mac eventually went ashore to make a broadcast, saying, "People of the Philippines, I have returned..." As Mac says in his memoir, two years earlier uttering, "I shall return" wasn't planned, it came on the spur of the moment, showing his natural talent for rhetoric. Mac's eloquence strikes me as more effective than that of another *grandseigneur* at the time, Churchill, who tended to go a bit too far in flowery language, at least in writing. Regarding the book format, Mac's memoir is very succinct yet immensely readable.

***

The Battle of the Philippines had only just begun. The Japanese, in the summer having been shocked by the fall of Saipan, a substantial Pacific island with a large Japanese population, decided that wherever the Americans attacked next it would be the decisive battle, a time for a main defensive Japanese effort. All available resources would be put in – and when it turned out to be the Philippines all remaining naval and aerial forces were summoned. And eventually, on 20-21 October, there took place a naval battle over the greater part of the archipelago, at one time close to inflict a major tactical defeat on the US. It wouldn't have been able to turn the war – because, a US naval replacement program having been in the pipe since long now began to have full effect, leaving Japan far behind in terms of naval tonnage.

It could never catch up. However, operationally Japan still was to be counted on. Among other things they now sacrificed their super battleship *Musashi* to attract US naval aircraft, at the same time as another task force sailed eastwards towards Leyte and a third force arrived from north of the island. Next, the latter force succeeded in dragging Halsey's carrier group away from the Philippines. The Japanese task forces would meet and strike at the invasion fleet at Leyte; however, the one on the eastern course by Mindanao Strait had to run the gauntlet by way of an American force, and the Kurita force coming from the north could harass Sprague's force for a while but it didn't lead to any decisive situation. So, Kurita soon decided to leave the area and sail north again.

However, just when Sprague's force believed that the danger was over, another part of the Japanese plan went into effect. For now, the US Navy at Leyte was attacked by *kamikaze aircraft* – suicide attacks from the sky. Japan, with a "decisive battle, total war" concept, had set up suicide squadrons in the land-based naval air groups and in the Philippines, this arm became operational for the first time, at Leyte specifically. The plan was to interact with the fleets which were believed to be in battle contact with the US fleet near Leyte – and indeed, the US force was now a little shaken up and believing that the worst was over. Then the kamikaze squadrons arrived, they duly attacked some select ships and sank one and damaged one. The sunk vessel was the escort aircraft carrier *St. Lo* which had a wooden deck, permitting the diving Mitsubishi Zero to actually penetrate it and explode with its bomb in the vital internal structure of the ship, sinking it. Tactically, this was a success and encouraged the Japanese to use kamikaze squadrons from now on and to the end of the war.

It was an intense phase of the Pacific War but the Leyte operation could not be stopped: 6th Army under Walter Krueger was still ashore, Sprague's fleet had defended itself against continuous kamikaze attacks and the Japanese fleet had received a blow from which it could not recover. For Mac, the Leyte gamble had succeeded. Soon the strategic heartland of the Philippines was taken; Mac landed with two armies on Luzon in January 1945 and could enter

Manila in February. The fighting was hard and the Japanese sold themselves dearly: *the Japs were hard to kill* as an official report had it. The Americans could free their comrades who had been in prison since the capitulation on Bataan in May 1942. MacArthur could walk around in a devastated Manila as a liberator, for instance revisiting the apartment which he had rented there before the war, now totally devastated. Later US forces took Iwo Jima and Okinawa as steps toward an invasion of mainland Japan but the dropping of the atomic bombs rendered this unnecessary. US Navy and the Marines had been at the forefront of the recent operations but FDR thought that the casualties had been too high, making him look more favorably on the Army. So, rightly or wrongly he gave the command of the occupation to the Army and placed MacArthur in charge of it all.

Japan had capitulated. MacArthur went to the country comparatively early, flying there in his personal C-54 staff plane "Bataan," which was seen by Churchill as one of the bravest acts of the war for there were still determined Japanese soldiers around, groomed in traditional concepts of Japan as a holy land, the land of the gods. But the plane landed outside of Tokyo and nothing tangibly dramatic happened, Mac was brought to the city in a motorcade and the only strange thing was that the road taken was guarded by lined-up Japanese soldiers having their backs to the road; however, this was not to be seen as a condescending gesture, it being the standard even when the Emperor was out riding in his car.

When Mac came to the city news of his arrival spread quickly and this created a great deal of goodwill, this move of virtually landing at the head of the invasion army and without a large escort when arriving at the country he would control. He had a feeling for *the proper gesture*, Mac, he knew what gave effect – and he above all knew that now he had to tread somewhat cautiously, Japan being so thoroughly defeated that it was crucial to win the hearts and minds of the people and not come across as a brutal invader. Of course, there was a pragmatic view behind this, seeing to it that the country would not swing over to communism and be a potential ally of the Soviet Union.

Pragmatism or not, Mac in Japan 1945 was the right man at the right time, and a mixture of soft and hard measures steered the country through this critical time. Now his rhetorical aptitude also came into its own, like after the capitulation ceremony on the USS Missouri in September holding a reasonably elevated speech with sweeping historical comparisons and thoughts on the future et cetera – and his words hit the right key, giving the impression of the *victor's generosity.* Conversely, can you imagine a Halsey or a Nimitz holding a similar speech? No, you can't, for the Navy lacked top men with a political sensibility similar of the one MacArthur had. The back side of this might be Mac's presidential ambitions and his "Caesarian" trait; for better or worse, he was an *American Caesar,* as the title of Marshall's bio has it. And imperial or not, the role of Mac in Japan 1945-50 was rather similar of the one of Commander Perry in the mid 19th century, arriving at the land in a time of transition and with the ability to steer the course for a new development.

10. GEORGE S. PATTON (1885-1945)

IN SWEDEN, WE KNOW HIM AS *Patton, Panzer General*. His full name was *George Smith Patton, Junior*. He was the third of the same name, George Smith Patton I being a lawyer from Virginia who participated on the Confederate side of the civil war, falling in battle as a colonel. His son, George Smith Patton II, also chose the military path and attended the famous Virginia Military Institute, but because of the hard times, he must become a lawyer instead. With time, he moved with his family to California where he became the manager of a large estate. And so, in 1885 was born George Smith Patton III, "our" Patton. He, too, was to attend VMI; when he would order his uniform from the tailor it turned out that he had the exact same dimensions as both father and grandfather had. He was a long and slender type, fair-haired and with small teeth.

After VMI followed West Point which he, in the end, graduated from, despite problems of dyslexia. Patton began his career in the cavalry, in these pre-war times an aristocratic stronghold. In 1912, he participated in the Stockholm Olympics in the military pentathlon, doing well in the diverse branches except for pistol marksmanship. He blamed it on the fact that the bright northern summer nights had disturbed his sleep. He ended up in fifth place.

Patton participated in the punitive expedition to Mexico, militarily rather insignificant but an important career step. Next came the participation in WWI where Patton chose to serve in the new branch of *armored troops,* the mechanized form of cavalry stressing movement. He led the setting up of two battalions, a force created completely from scratch. Patton had strict demands on discipline and tidiness. He even delved into the technical side of the phenomenon and learned to drive a tank. With time this force could be deployed in the combat zone which was in the battle for the St. Mihiel salient, a large angle shaped front bulge in Lorraine which the AEF was given the task to wipe out. It was in August 1918 and the battle that ensued was not particularly dramatic; however, in war, nothing should be taken lightly. Patton, then a lieutenant colonel, led his tank brigade and fulfilled his task. In September it was inserted into the Meuse-Argonne-sector; during a particular attack Patton's tanks were knocked out or got lost so the crews had to attack on foot. In this process, Patton was hit in the thigh by a grapeshot. He was evacuated from the front and was soon rehabilitated but by then, the war had ended. He was in the fire for merely four days and he had expected more, so from now on he went hoping for a new war. His prayers would be answered even if it took more than twenty years.

In the inter-war years, Patton soldiered on in diverse army assignments, like designing a new cavalry saddle. However, the days of the horse were over, US Army stopped using them in the 30s, a sad day for the cavalry fan Patton, seeing the service branch of Custer, Sheridan, and Stuart simply disappear. However, the spirit of the cavalry was taken over by the tank arm which Patton knew about. Experimenting with tanks at the HQ and General Staff School at Fort Leavenworth, with Eisenhower as an ally, Patton toyed with the idea of independent, offensive armored units. They would not merely be a support for the infantry. But the time wasn't ready for this in the United States and Patton didn't rock the boat, he would not be a martyr for an unpopular idea. But after the German success against France 1940 the question of separate, strategic armored units was high on the agenda – and when US Army finally organized its armored divisions and corps Patton was one of the driving forces in the process. WWII thus had already begun in Europe and the United States was not yet a belligerent but it had started to plan a rearmament, inter alia on the army side. A legendary exercise in Louisiana 1940 tested the new ideas of mechanized warfare and a training center was set up in the Arizona desert to study armor issues. American tank designs were launched, like M3 Stuart, Sherman, and Lee/Grant, designed to meet the German Panzer III and IV on the battlefield.

War was looming and this suited Patton well. Among other things he by this time wrote a letter to Eisenhower with the wording: "Let us hope for a long and *bloody* war!" This was Patton, he loved war and made no secret·of it. Another example of this was when he visited Paris after the liberation in 1944 and he was invited to dinner with a colleague and some ladies. On the question of why they were officers the colleague said that it was to fight for peace, justice, and democracy while Patton doubted this, do you really believe in that, isn't it so that you're an officer because you love to fight...?

Let's get ahead a bit, to the autumn of 1942. Then the Allied Powers, equal to the UK and the USA, as its first common ground operation had selected North Africa as a theater. A landing on the European continent loomed but the coalition lacked the required fifty divisions for that; instead, a lower threshold was offered by a landing in North Africa. In this theater, while in the East the Brits pushed Rommel back from Libya, a combined UK-US force was landed in Morocco and Algeria. Patton, however, played no significant part in the landings proper, and once in Morocco focused on planning the subsequent landings on Sicily.

The Brits led by Montgomery pushed on from the east and the new force from the west, soon trapping Rommel in Tunisia. But it wasn't over yet. Rommel went on sick leave and his replacement, Hans von Arnim, in March 1943 launched a counterattack against the Americans, the 2nd Army Corps under General Fredendall. It was taken by surprise at the Kasserine Pass, battalion after battalion being routed. Eisenhower, commander over the allies in western North Africa, dismissed Fredendall, a man having let command and discipline go adrift while he built a bomb safe HQ in a remote valley. They must install Patton instead; Eisenhower called his friend in Morocco and asked him to come and shape up the show.

The change would immediately come about. On 7 March Patton entered the small Tunisian village of Djebel Kouif where 2nd Army Corps had its headquarters. It was a motorcade with armored cars and half-tracks, it was sirens and horns and it was Patton himself wearing riding boots, a helmet with two clearly visible stars and a revolver with ebony inlays. He stepped out of his car, slammed with a whip against the boot shaft and stepped into the HQ. And at once he launched his new regime meaning that every soldier must from now on always wear helmet, gaiters and tie, the "gaiters and tie" element rather useless in combat but symbolically important, saying to all and sundry that a new general was now in command.

A counter-attack was also planned. In this, the task of the Americans was only to threaten the German flank, while the main task of driving the Germans from the so-called *Mareth line* in southern Tunisia was given to Montgomery's 8th Army. Patton's 2nd Army Corps was included in the British 1st Army under General Sir Harold Alexander who looked down on the Americans, he considered them to be "physically and mentally weakened newcomers"; therefore, they were given the limited task to threaten the enemy in the flank. Alexander may have had some justice for his contempt, the Yanks had indeed been beaten at Kasserine, but at the same time, he was something of an imperialist subconsciously realizing that the days of the Empire were over and that the Americans were the new global hegemony, Alexander compensating this with a haughty, superior attitude. Patton, on the other hand, thought nothing of Alexander, privately noting that *he has an unusually small head* which could explain things...

2nd Army Corps would perform a flank attack to support 8th Army and on 17 March it began. The Germans retreated in good order and withdrew from the Kasserine Pass, however, having a surprise in store on 23 March when the Germans attacked the US 1st Division, "Big Red One" of WWI fame, now under Patton's overall command. The Yanks were in dire straits but held their ground, in the evening managing to stem the deluge. Afterward, Patton could note that his shake-up had caused a result, the soldiers having bitten the bullet, not giving ground. No one had fled and all the fallen were lying with their heads in the front direction. It was a considerable improvement since Kasserine.

The battles continued to the end of March and the beginning of April and it went forward but the decisive blow would not come, the Germans instead retreating in good order up the Tunisian east coast. Eisenhower then decided that Omar Bradley would take over 2nd Corps while Patton continued to plan the Sicilian invasion, which he had dealt with before replacing Fredendall. In the coming Sicilian landing, Patton would lead 7th Army, made up of 2nd Corps plus another corps. The landings were done in the fashion of a concentrated assault in the south, Monty, the overall commander, preferring this safe option in favor of landing battle groups all around the island which would risk them being defeated one by one. However, this main effort in the south also meant that the Germans could retreat over the island in rather good order. Monty had foreseen this but his plan was rather sound, a plan of the "better safe than sorry" kind.

Patton, for his part, was rather active in assisting his army in the landings, the D-Day of 11 July being the first day of the war he felt that he had earned his salary. He was there, on the beaches, in the proximity of danger, a way to see if he "still had it," if he had the guts to be in the combat zone proper. Resistance was relatively substantial, there were German armored elites on the enemy side, not Vichy French as during the Morocco landings in 1942, but generally, the Americans and Brits came ashore and in the evening Patton could look back on a good day's work. He had been in the fire, he had made a difference, he was a warrior having come home. The frustration from the peace years began to wane. Then the invasion rolled on and, on 22 July, Palermo was taken, the first European capital to be taken by the Allies. Patton and Eisenhower celebrated by having C-Rations in the city hall. As intimated the whole of Sicily soon fell in the Allies' hands with the Germans retreating in good order, escaping to the Italian mainland.

The Italian campaign was a long and drawn-out affair, rather uninteresting from an operational point of view. As for Patton, his future was in jeopardy by this time because of "the slapping incident". When inspecting a field hospital Patton approached a shell-shocked private whom he wanted to "shake up," elevate from lethargy, by slapping him with his glove. This only made matters worse. The incident caused a public outcry when it became known. Patton must apologize to the man and the hospital staff. This put his career in jeopardy, though the outcome was only that he would remain a three-star general (Lieutenant General), never being promoted General or General of the Army. It was a high price for a slap but probably right, there must be limits to how a general behaves. You must display some judgment, must be able to behave with some decency, in addition to being able to fight the enemy.

All told, Patton was saved by having friends in high places, like Eisenhower and soon even Roosevelt. Despite the pressure from the public the President chose to keep his general, citing Lincoln's words about Grant: "I can't spare this man; he fights." The lethargic, over-cautious spirit that Fredendall symbolized, was still quite common in the US Army in those days. Patton was there to instill fighting spirit and "get up and go", to boldly advance in cavalry style, penetrate to the depth and disrupt all of the enemy's distribution. Operationally, they needed to break the backbone of the Wehrmacht. The German was still a formidable opponent, he had battle experience and several divisions to defend the European mainland. It *was* in a sense a "Fortress Europe," a *Festung Europa* – and it would not be taken with myopic, outdated combat attitudes shaped by the siege battles of WWI.

In the meantime, the allies had moved on to take Italy, an operation Patton had nothing to do with, the US operation there being led by General Mark Clark. Instead, Patton was given orders to go to England to start building 3rd Army, along with 1st Army forming the Normandy landings American army group led by Bradley. Patton took part in this by for instance traveling round and holding rousing speeches, saying things like, "It's not about going out dying for your country, it's to get the other dumb bastard dying for *his* country!" Patton had a real talent for the stage, and one of many anecdotes d'Este gives in his bio is when Patton in his field HQ once was visited by Bob Hope and another comedian, in the ensuing dinner conversation Patton's spirits running high, reducing the professional actors to mere *straight men*. I'd say, there is no general figure like Patton in any of the armies that fought in WWII: a fighter at heart but also, for better or worse, an inspired actor and joker.

3rd Army was ready for battle. The actual landing beaches were to be taken by 1st Army, which it did on 6 June 1944. Then, at the end of July, 3rd Army had been shipped over to make a breakthrough and pursue the enemy relentlessly, never giving him a quiet moment. This was Patton at his best: it was material to keep the offensive going and make deep inroads, using armored divisions strategically. The Yanks surely had the odds on their side for after the breakthrough at Avranches the Germans didn't have much to put up against the US air and ground forces. But, at the same time, Patton deserves credit for doing his thing in this situation, the US Army spirit as intimated still being characterized by a conservative mentality; a man like Marshall could certainly argue that this war was different from that of the static First World War battles, but the ordinary general had not yet taken this to heart, he lived with the mud of Flanders as his *inner image of war,* his *tactical subconscious,* his archetypal form of war shaping his concept of combat. In this, Patton's cavalry spirit was needed to shake up things, like telling his generals to bypass certain points and leave them to the infantry, driving them to advance a little further than what they thought was possible. It was once again the Napoleonic dictum of, *"Audace, audace, de l'activité".* Before the war, Patton had fought this war in his mind and now he could project this vision in the real world. He gained ground, defeated enemies and took cities, being lauded by both the French and the US public back home.

The Allies broke through and encircled large German units, reached the Seine and liberated Paris. Brits and Americans fought side by side against Germany. In September the pace of advancement went down, due to the Allied lines of supply lengthening and the German supply lines in equal measure shortening. For the 3rd Army, the new rhythm was symbolized by being bogged down before Metz. It was only taken by the end of November. Soon after the 3rd Army reached the river Saar, meaning it had contact with German territory. But in the meantime the Germans had built up reserves for a surprise, with two panzer armies planning to break up the American part of the front, separating 3rd Army from its 1st Army neighbor and eventually reaching Antwerp whose port would be blocked. With this Hitler wanted to gain time, stopping the allied offensive in the West to be able to concentrate on the Eastern Front. As it turned out the Germans in this offensive would never reach Antwerp, there was never any enduring strategic success, but the *strategic surprise* was indeed effective, and during the first week of the offensive the Allies were shaken in their self-confidence. They learned that war is never a one-sided business, it is a duel with blows and counter-blows.

The German attack was launched on 16 December. The German tank spearheads could easily break through and overrun the handful of weak divisions Hodges, 1st Army commander, had grouped in the wooded and mountainous Ardennes. The readiness was low, no one expecting a German counterthrust of this caliber. On 17 December Patton, for his part, learned that there was something going on in this sector to the north of 3rd Army; already now he seems to have made the outlines for an attack on the German southern flank, soon to be affected by 4th Armored Division going off to relieve Bastogne. On the same day, Patton met with Eisenhower who ordered Patton to make a counter attack of the implied type. Patton is said to have surprised Ike with the answer that he could get going on 22 December. It was no easy task for 3rd Army to make such a change of direction, a logistic challenge in wintry climes and on slippery roads.

However, the strategic relief force was set to go on the promised date, at the same time as the Germans had continued their progress.

It was above all their current, southern panzer army having had successes, inter alia by the bypass and encirclement of Bastogne, Belgium. A lot of American troops were trapped there. In any case, Patton's units mounted their Sherman tanks and half-tracks, the latter loaded with infantry in olive green lumber jacket, steel helmet on the head, tie knot, gaiters buckled, and M-1 carbines loaded. The first obstacle they encountered was a German "Parachute Division." They were no elite, mostly consisting of quickly trained air force ground crews, which struck out a few American tanks with anti-tank guns and assault guns. But when a certain armor colonel named Creighton Abram went to action on Christmas day a decisive move was made, taking a village where the armor force had been stuck and routing the Parachute Division.

The next day was launched the 11 km long journey to Bastogne with an armored battle group of only 20 tanks. In the afternoon at 5 o'clock was established contact with the American infantry in Bastogne and soon Abrams could shake hands with the commander of 101st Airborne, Tony McAuliffe. He had continued to fight against the Germans during the entire time he had been encircled. In response to a request to capitulate, he had, for example, replied, "Nuts!"

The relief of Bastogne was not the only battle in the Ardennes by this time, but it was of great symbolic value. Patton, who ultimately was responsible for the counterstrike, was hailed as a hero, inter alia with the newspaper caption, *"PATTON, of course."* There was indeed the need for a hero after the initial backlash of this event but the praise was justified nonetheless. Patton acted spontaneously and intuitively at the news that something was going on, he at once envisioned a counterstrike, and when Ike ordered him to do it he could directly implement it. After the Ardennes, Patton could go on with his reputation bolstered while Bradley and Hodges had their reputations tarnished.

The battle for the Ardennes continued for many weeks but on 29 January the front line was restored, the bulge was eradicated. However, the Germans had been retreating relatively undisturbed.

3rd Army could now enter Germany proper; first across the border it was *not,* for that achievement was done by 1st Army via the undamaged Hindenburg Bridge at Remagen, advance units going over the Rhine on 7 March. Patton's army crossed the river on 22 March in the Eifel region. Then it continued to occupy Southern Germany and now it was not the case of notable operations anymore, the Germans surrendering after predominantly symbolic battles.

The war was over and Patton became the commander of the 12th Army, which wasn't an army but only staff with the task of writing a history of the war. Patton spent the time to write a kind of memoir, *War as I Knew It,* composed of diary notes from the autumn of 1942 to the summer 1945 as well as general lessons. Patton had thought of giving it the sub-caption: "Helpful Hints for Hopeful Heroes"...

The fighting in Europe was over and Patton was bored. He volunteered to fight in the Pacific as a divisional commander but it was not to be. So he spent the days doing things like hunting and this was how he died. It was a day in December 1945 when he was going to hunt for pheasants in the Palatinate, going in his spacious pre-war Cadillac. The driver for some reason didn't see a truck in front of them making a left-hand turn; the Cadillac slammed into its side and Patton was severely injured in the crash while his ADC and driver were rather unharmed. Patton proved to be paralyzed from the waist down, his neck broken. For a week he lingered between life and death, knowing that this was the end; he said, "This is a helluva way to die..." He died in his sleep on 21 December 1945.

A summary of Patton's life must again underline that he was indispensable for the Allies because few generals had the offensive spirit that Patton personified. Few generals had his ability to lift his eyes from a given situation and look beyond the horizon. Despite the fact that the offensive armor tactic was established a bit into WWII it took time for the Allies to digest the lessons.

On the American side, Patton was the man to nurture and spread this spirit, the spearheading spirit. He was that spirit; he lived it.

Patton was complex. One anecdote that d'Este supplies us with is from some nurses visiting his HQ. When they are all going for a walk in the countryside, the nurses suddenly see Patton dropping to his knees and praying. It may be hypocrisy to pray publicly like this but Patton didn't care, he acted on the spur of the moment and his creed was true in that respect. He also read the Bhagavad-Gîtâ and believed in reincarnation. *There were many sides to the man...*

11. DWIGHT D. EISENHOWER (1893-1968)

THIS WAS HIS FINEST HOUR: the time before the D-Day 1944. Then, namely, *Dwight David Eisenhower* went around and spoke to the units which would participate in the invasion, and in doing this he sometimes gathered the men around him for more informal chats. This, Marshall later said, was a stroke of genius, it was a gesture creating a bond to the commander in the heart of the simplest G. I. Joe. Going around and meeting every unit like this was also done by Rommel on his side of the canal at the time – and in this, Ernst Jünger said, was revealed an archaic trait, that of the commander before the battle going to see every soldier, fostering the spirit of, "we're all in it together".

Eisenhower would lead the invasion even if the main military plans were drawn up by Montgomery who had previously not been so impressed by Ike as a military commander, his inexperience did show—for he hadn't participated in WWI, not in a combat capacity—and he hadn't seen any dead on a battlefield until the North Africa campaign in 1942. This campaign Ike led as General-in-Chief and prior to this, he was head of the American military mission to England, forming an American invasion army together with the British one. With time, he became supreme commander for this entire *Operation Overlord,* head of Americans and Brits, navy, air force and the army. And even if he was a little inexperienced in the beginning he got better with time; even Montgomery saw him grow with the task, just before D-day realizing that they had selected the right man for the job, a rock of a man which would not waver in the trial. And Ike's decision to launch the operation despite some weather problem was an example of him being of "the right stuff," for the weather soon improved and everything went largely as planned.

After the war, Ike was promoted *General of the Army* (five-star general) and commander of the then equivalent of the Joint Chiefs of Staff, a post he held from December 1945 to October 1947. In 1948 he retired and wrote his memoirs, *Crusade in Europe,* and we see the political positioning here; already now he may have hoped to be nominated as Republican presidential candidate but the place was instead given to a certain Thomas Dewey, so Eisenhower had to find something else to do. He became Director for Columbia University in New York, followed by the time as NATO manager in Paris 1951-52. At that time its headquarters was situated in this city before De Gaulle, in a nationalist gesture, opted out of NATO in peacetime and bade the organization to move, NATO thus ending up in Brussels in 1967.

Soon, in 1952, Ike really did receive the Republican nomination for presidential candidate. Outwardly Ike was a bit reluctant—but—it wouldn't be so bold to suggest that he also wanted to become president. The phenomenon of *generals who become presidents* is a little controversial, for according to a certain tradition (established by the German military reformer von Moltke, late 19th century) generals should only devote themselves to their profession and avoid politics. That may be a fine ambition in itself. But – there is also a thing called *responsibility* and if a general finds himself in a situation where the land needs his talent to rule, then he mustn't shrink from it, referring to some obscure tradition. A general having *democratic* political ambitions, aiming to act in accordance with the rules of the game, is fully sound. Conversely, the famous dictum of Sherman— "if nominated I will not run, if elected I will not serve"—mustn't be the final word in this complex. And in the US context, we have seen generals like Washington, Andrew Jackson, William Harrison, Zachary Taylor and Grant having become presidents so the career path is established in American history. Grant has been treated earlier in this book, and concerning Washington, he had a rather substantial military career in the French and Indian War and of course the War of Liberation. As for the others, *Andrew Jackson* was president in the 1830s; he had no formal military training but during the War of 1812 he was the head of the US force at New Orleans, winning a major victory over the English which gave Jackson the reputation of a hero, a veritable plus-weapon in the presidential campaign. "Old Hickory" was his nickname.

In the 1840s *William H. Harrison* was president, a general having won a battle against the Indians in the state of Indiana; it was the battle of Tippecanoe and then Harrison was nominated by the Whig party with John Tyler as vice-presidential candidate, endowed with the campaign song with the chorus: "Tippecanoe and Tyler too, Tippecanoe and Tyler too"... Harrison caught a cold after having held his inaugural speech in a snowstorm, he died shortly after and Tyler had to assume office. A relative of Harrison was president at the end of the nineteenth century, Benjamin Harrison, but he wasn't a general.

In 1849 *Zachary Taylor* was inaugurated as president. Even before the above mentioned Moltke instigated tradition of officers avoiding politics, he was an example of such a non-political military man for he had never voted. Militarily, he had distinguished himself as the leader of the northern army in the Mexican War; the southern army, led by Winfield Scott, was landed at Vera Cruz and having, for instance, Robert E. Lee serving in it.

Two Civil War generals who became presidents were, for their part, *Hayes* and *Rutherford*, Republicans both as well as Grant before them, the good general who was a rather poor president. Outgoing President Truman referred to the latter and forecast that Ike would become "a new Grant," a competent general who gets lost in policy and leads a corrupt administration. But it didn't turn out that badly. Ike defeated the Democrat Adlai Stevenson and was a decent president, major scandals didn't occur and the administration was not like Grant's. Ike may have become a bit senile at the end of his second term (he had also suffered one or two heart attacks, hidden to the public at the time). However, he also introduced the practice of having a *chief of staff* to handle the daily, practical agenda of the President, a military style function when leading divisions and upwards. Of course, some kind of "chancery clerk/office manager" function had been around before in handling the presidency but this move of Eisenhower's befitted "the Imperial Presidency," for better or worse.

Pros and cons of Ike: as a person he had charm but he could also have fits of anger. That he had a temperament was human, it mustn't be totally held against him, but it should be noted that he wasn't all smiles. Further, in the Vietnam issue he was a hawk; in this respect, we can note the attitudes of Marshall (leaving all kinds of politics after retirement) and MacArthur (advising against the deployment of American troops on the Asian mainland).

An interesting detail of the Eisenhower gestalt is his puritanical background in Kansas where he was born and his mother was active in *the Mennonites,* a sect formed by the German immigrant Menno Simon. It came to be related to the Amish sect, the Midwest-based movement living a pious farmer life on the nineteenth-century level. That Eisenhower, the man who is said to have threatened the Koreans with atomic weapons in order to put an end to the Korean War, almost had Amish background; this is rather interesting.

Ike was born in 1890, graduated from West Point in 1915 and remained in the United States during WWI, among other things as an instructor at the artillery shooting range the army had in the region of the old Gettysburg battlefield. In 1925 he attended the general staff school in Fort Leavenworth and 1929-1939 he was stuck in a career-wise dead end, being a staff major under MacArthur, first assisting Mac in the army chief function and then in the Philippines appointment. Ike wasn't so keen on this, his career went nowhere working for the Caesarian MacArthur, but orders were orders. When Eisenhower later would record TV advertising for his presidential candidacy he said to the TV people that this would probably go well; he had attended drama school for ten years, "The MacArthur School of Dramatic Arts"...

When Ike returned to the States in the 1940s he became, among other things, the commander of a regiment. One day he would inspect the kitchen; he became hungry so while he was there he took up a handful of minced meat and a raw onion and chewed on these while inspecting. A chef who saw the whole said, "Now *there's* a tough guy!" This is told by Stephen E. Ambrose in his biography, a telling detail indeed.

12. OMAR N. BRADLEY (1893-1981)

STYLE-WISE, A GENERAL CAN BE MANY things as long as he is victorious. For instance, a bespectacled teetotaller may not be the archetypal warrior type but there has been this kind of general too. Like *Omar Nelson Bradley*.

In this case, "teetotaller" might need to be clarified. Bradley's wife was indeed of the temperance kind and Bradley himself didn't taste any kind of liquor until he was about 30. But he was not completely against alcoholic beverages; during the battles on the Cotentin peninsula in 1944 American troops stumbled upon a large stash of wine and spirits, and as head of the 1st Army Bradley was offered part of it. He chose a few bottles of champagne, to be used at the christening of his grandson. If the child would be baptized *in* the champagne, we do not know.

Bradley may have been "a *bon générale ordinaire*," a steady workman, a tad mediocre but he had the ability to learn from his mistakes. Like, when working alongside Montgomery in Normandy Bradley knew that he Brit was the senior partner, the more experienced general. For instance, sometime after the D-day landings in 1944 the Americans got bogged down by the stern German defense in the landscape partitioned by shrubbery (*bocage*). Bradley asked Monty what he, Bradley, did wrong – and then Monty placed his index finger and middle finger together on a place on the map, saying, "You have to concentrate your forces – like this."

Bradley listened and then started planning the outbreak at Avranches.

An important element of the plan which emerged, in this case, was *strategic bombing*: US Army had used it before for this kind of tactical support, inter alia in the battle of Monte Cassino, and now it would be tried again although the method didn't work so well in Italy. Bradley would also focus on the interaction between infantry and armor, and with time this all evolved into the plan for *Operation Cobra*, aimed at making a breakout from the Normandy bridgehead. This was also known as the outbreak at Avranches.

To break the German front line Bradley decided to use aerial bombing on a massive scale; strategic bombers of the type B-24 Liberator would concentrate their effort on a 0.5 x 1 km wide area, hereinafter referred to as the "carpet" because the tactics in question were called *carpet bombing*. The approach would be done along a road which ran in parallel with the front line, the road from Lessay on the coast via Périers to St. Lo. After the bombs had been dropped and struck out the enemy troops on the small surface, two infantry divisions would break through and secure the flanks of the breach. Then one motorized and two armored divisions would go through the gap; the first division would take the town of Coutances, 24 km to the south, and the other two Avranches on the coast, in the corner where Normandy and Brittany meet. The latter objective was the most important thing for well beyond Avranches the Americans would have *operational freedom*. They would be out in a more free, unbounded terrain, not hemmed in by the Normandy shrubs and brushwood. Put differently, if American reinforcements were inserted in the expected gap the German left flank would be unhinged, it would be overrun and turned. The main part of the reinforcements would be Patton's 3rd Army, the intended second echelon after 1st Army had taken the Normandy beaches and then some.

It was in the middle of July and the general situation was gloomy: a previous attack against Coutances had failed, further to the east Montgomery had got stuck in front of Caen, the weather was cloudy which made aerial operations impossible and the whole situation was reminiscent of WWI with stagnation and frustration. The plan Bradley was beginning to execute was only known by a few; however, the Germans guessed that their left flank was in danger so they sent two armored divisions from the Caen region to the western, "American" part of the front line.

The bomb attack would have started on 21 July but the weather was bad so it had to be postponed. On 24 July, the bomb armada finally took off from its bases in England but 20 minutes before H Hour it received the order to turn back because the weather hadn't cleared as expected. Some bombers, however, had already completed their mission but they happened to bomb blue force troops several kilometers behind the designated objective, the carpet of 0.5 x 1 km. How they had been able to drop their bombs behind the carpet perplexed Bradley because he had designated the objective with the east-west road as an approach, indicating a course parallel to the front line, you can't miss it... It was soon found out that the planes hadn't taken this route, instead, they had been flying in from the north, this being the shortest route from their bases in England. The bomb command even said that they must take this route even the next day or else it all had to be canceled.

Bradley's troops were only 1.5 km behind the target so he took a huge risk. But he let the bomb command have its way; it had in fact already dropped bombs on the carpet, the intention was out, so Bradley had to keep going. On 25 July a major effort was made, with high altitude bombers, medium bombers and fighter-bombers all morning bombing the carpet, again having some blue forces killed in the process, some hundred GI's, reportedly leading to the decision to never again use strategic bombing for tactical purposes in this war.

Due to blue forces losses, it took some time to get the ground attack going. But the attack did eventually get rolling, the enemy in the carpet had been virtually obliterated and 24 hours after starting Bradley knew that it would be a success. On 27 July was reached Coutances, the primary objective of the infantry division, at the same time as the armored divisions headed for Avranches farther south. On 1 August the corner down to Brittany had been turned and at the same time, Patton had arrived at the site to take command of the forces which would be 3rd Army. Until then only the US 1st Army was on the site, commanded by Bradley; with 3rd Army having also arrived an army group was formed, led by Bradley who handed over 1st Army command to Cortney Hodges.

Patton forged ahead, it was about striking into the depth of the enemy distribution and disrupt it completely and in this, speed was essential. However, in this, he also exposed his left flank. The Germans duly attacked this but since the Allies had aerial superiority this German panzer thrust was quelled, drowned in a deluge of tactical air force firepower. The American spearhead wasn't cut off, Gunther von Kluge didn't reach the sea.

The counterattack failed. By a double envelopment, the rest of the German Normandy force became encircled in August, the Battle of the Falaise Pocket, the Brits coming in from the north and the Yanks from the west and south. Supplemented by aerial bombing the German losses were 50,000 dead and lots of heavy equipment lost. Only scattered remains of the units managed to get out of the encirclement. Two German panzer armies had been eradicated by the Allies. At the same time as the Falaise Pocket operation, the Americans continued to channel troops down western Normandy via the breach Bradley had effected, Patton's armored troops thus clearing most of mid-France. Also, the Brits and Canadians finally got going on their wing; the Allies had definitely broken the deadlock and managed to break out of the Normandy bridgehead where they had been prisoners for so long, over a month. Operation Cobra had succeeded. In fact, it led to a general offensive that did not halt until reaching the German border in the autumn.

As intimated, strategic bombing for tactical purposes wasn't used anymore in WWII. But it was employed in every major American conflict afterward – in Korea, Vietnam and The Gulf War of 1991. It is something of "a blunt force," imprecise. However, an all-out ban on this method doesn't seem to be forthcoming in the US doctrine – though it might be that the overall era of carpet bombing is over, along with the American propensity for invading countries in imperial style.

The rest of Bradley's warpath in Europe isn't so shiny. He didn't fail completely but neither did he come out with flying colors. He was surprised in the Ardennes (see the Patton chapter) and the rest of the operations until the end of the war were conducted in an ordinary, lackluster fashion. However, there wasn't so much room for maneuver so it's easy to be critical.

Bradley was an ordinary general, fine in the everyday handling of affairs but unprepared for the unexpected. Then you might say that his overall "cold" was needed along Patton's "fire". Well, maybe. We will only end this chapter with another comparison between the two: in the handling of subordinate generals.

Patton only relieved one (1) of his subordinate generals of command during WWII: Orlando Ward. Bradley, on the other hand, acting in sync with an army directive from Eisenhower, fired generals rather often. Patton, the symbol of impulsiveness, was rather patient in dealing with his generals. He educated them. This we see in d'Este's bio.

Talking about bios, the source of Bradley's war in this chapter is his autobiography *A Soldier's Story*. And it's a good read because of its low-key style, its relative lack of bold statements and dashing moves. It depicts the land of infantry warfare: a down-to-earth fighting style focused on limited objectives.

13. CLAIRE LEE CHENNAULT (1893-1958)

I N TEXAS IN 1893 A CHILD WAS BORN named *Claire Lee Chennault.* The middle name had its background in his mother being a relative of Robert E. Lee. Chennault later joined the army and went through flight training in 1919, serving as a fighter pilot in the peacetime army of the 1920s. By this time, there was no independent air force; it was part of the army as "US Army Air Corps," later to be renamed "US Army Air Force" and finally, in 1947, becoming a separate service branch as "US Air Force". For his part, Chennault was a keen parachutist, a pioneer in the United States for setting up parachute troops; however, US Army wasn't so enthusiastic about this phenomenon while on the other hand, the Russians contacted Chennault to learn more about it. Eventually, the Soviet Union set up the first regular parachute troops.

In the American air force by this time there was a debate on whether the fighter or the bomber would dominate the future of air warfare. The bomber won it. The "common knowledge" of the 30s was that the bombers would always get through to the enemy capital and destroy it with bombs from the sky. Thus, promoters of the primacy of fighter aircraft like Chennault were a bit side-stepped. However, for this man, a new hope loomed on the eastern horizon – because, now Chennault was recruited as top flight instructor of the Chinese Air Force. He arrived in China in 1937, roughly at the time when Japan attacked the country so Chennault landed directly in the fray. He virtually became Chinese air force commander *de facto,* leading the Chinese aerial operations of the war.

In the beginning, the Chinese only had a marginal air force with double-decker bombers like Northrop 2EC while the enemy, the Japanese, had more modern planes of their own production. The Chinese leader by this time was Chiang Kai-Shek (pedants might want it spelled "Jiang Jeshi"); he came up with the idea that China would buy modern American planes for its air force and hire American pilots to fly them, like an aerial Foreign Legion. FDR OK'd the idea, however, only letting Chiang buy 100 planes, not the intended 500. The type was Curtiss P-40 B, a low-winged, single-seat fighter with an inline engine, one of the best planes of its kind though not *the* best.

With time Chennault became the commander of this air force, leading it in operations against the Japanese in Burma and southern China. But I'm getting ahead; the unit was organized in the spring of 1941 and most crucially, it had to have pilots to fly the planes. And Chennault had no part in the recruitment per se. For this, special agents toured the air force bases in the US asking pilots if they would like to come and fly in China. However, the agents were not always welcome, some base commanders believing they were spies or charlatans and simply chasing them away. But in general, the recruitment went well, gathering the approximately 100 men needed, even if the unit never came to dispose of more than 60 aircraft. Now, the unit was named *Air Volunteer Group* and was divided into three units, *Panda Bears, Hell's Angels,* and *Adam and Eve.*

AVG would fly for China in its war against Japan, but when the pilots arrived in Asia the operational task had changed slightly. AVG ended up in the British colony of Burma since the machines that would be used were based there, intended for British use. However, the British now did a smart move: they let AVG use one of the airbases in the land, given that AVG assisted the British forces in the fight against the Japanese. Now it was December 1941 and Japan had extended the war to include the whole of south-east Asia; in addition to the United States and its bases Pearl Harbor and the Philippines, Holland's and England's Asian colonies including Burma were attacked. Thus, AVG partly ended up in the latter country and this

Chiang Kai-Shek had not counted on. But he agreed to it because the defense of Burma was important to the Nationalist Chinese territory he ruled, a territory now cut off from the sea in the east by the Japanese land offensive and thus in need of a back-door through Burma, symbolized in the Burma Road opened in 1939. The western powers could then send supplies to Burma, and via Rangoon and the Chinese provinces of Yunnan and Kweichow reach Sechuan and the capital Chungking, the heart of Nationalist China. It was in Chiang's interest to allow AVG to fight in Burma. But only one squadron would stay there while the other two were based in Kunming and Yunnan of China.

Chennault now was the head of the AVG, he was no longer merely an adviser to the Chinese air force. As such he developed tactics for his Flying Tigers, where, for example, dive attack was a great way for the heavy Curtiss machine to approach the lighter Mitsubishi Zero; acrobatic air combat should be avoided for in this, the Zero was superior. On the image side, AVG now painted shark teeth on their planes, after seeing some British P-40s in the Western Desert sporting this design – and it caught on propaganda-wise, AVG becoming known as "the Flying Tigers". They even commissioned Disney Studios to design an emblem, ending up having a rampant tiger tearing up a Japanese flag. The first three months after Pearl Harbor AVG fought a rather heroic fight against the Japanese war machine, they were seemingly the only ones standing against this apparently unstoppable offensive. It was among other things wild air combats over the Burmese capital Rangoon in the spring of 1942. Soon the city fell, the British army defending the colony on the ground retreated to its bases in India and AVG assisted in protecting this move. The fighters got embroiled in ground support which might not be optimal for this aircraft type but war is war.

Burma fell in the summer of 1942, the Japanese now being superior both on the ground and in the air. However, AVG had a high proportion of downed enemy planes per pilot, more than ten. The AVG pilots had earned their pay, the idea of having them in Burma was operationally sound – for, in addition, to harass the Japanese advance in Burma proper, AVG also assisted in denying the Japanese access to China from the west, along the crucial stretch of the Burma Road in the Salween Gorge. You could say that *one* of the reasons for the Japanese to attack East Asia in 1941 was bringing China to its knees, the operations in China having ground down to a halt after the promising beginning in 1937—and thus, one of the tasks of this "strike south"—option would be trying to take Nationalist China through the Salween back-door. But now the Japanese couldn't even take China from the rear so AVG was indeed taking part in crucial, strategically important operations.

In July 1942, the AVG was dissolved, apparently according to plan. During the more than six months of its existence, the unit had shot down 280 enemy planes against its own loss of 26 pilots, according to its own statistics. Some of the AVG pilots now went home to the States while others stayed in China to be US employed pilots in the air force now being set up in this region; this was called *China Air Task Force* and came to be headed by Chennault. Then, in 1943, it was subsumed under the 14th Air Force under general Bissell. Chennault, now with Brigadier-General rank, was only a subordinate commander of this force. But he had the ability to create a career in this remote area and the war was not over yet; Chennault may have been a somewhat odd figure but he knew how to communicate with HQs and politicians, somewhat in contrast to another American general in China, Joseph Stillwell of US Army, by this time fighting against the Japanese on the ground. Stilwell's wry and acerbic attitudes became a legend; however, he was right in stating that the Chinese war must be won on the ground, not by fancy air forces, and with the victory of Mao's communist guerrilla in 1949 he was proven right. The Americans tried to fight the communists with diverse mercenary-style air forces led by Chennault but it all came to naught.

By 1944 Chennault was back in American service in a US air force having changed quite remarkably since last: armadas of bombers supported by armadas of fighters, and at sea, aircraft carriers were the new strike weapon, replacing the battleship. As for 14th Air Force, its mission was to bomb Japan from Chinese bases, which wasn't so efficient. It was better to have bases in the Pacific, like Saipan and Tinian. As for fighting the Japanese in China nothing substantial happened; the land of the Rising Sun kept the territory it had held since 1937-38, that is, the coastal regions with the largest cities. This was the situation when the Japanese surrendered in August 1945. Then the Chinese Civil War flared up again, where the communists went from strength to strength while Chiang's nationalists had to retreat despite all the support of the USA.

What role did Claire Chennault play in this? He remained in China even after the war, even after in August 1945 taking leave from USAAF, for now, he would serve Chiang as head of a civil airway company, *China Air Transport* which later became the *Civil Air Transport* and lastly *Air America*. In the beginning, this company did services to the UN, like flying supplies to the north of China, part of humanitarian aid to people affected by the civil war, but later the company became more directly involved in the war. It is said that the US government through companies like this secretly supported Nationalist China, the US being formally neutral in the war. But in spite of all the investment of dollars, mediation and aid efforts the communists won and Chiang's forces retreated to Taiwan, still at the time of writing being a from Continental China independent state. When the Chinese Civil War was over it didn't take so long for Air America to get embroiled on the French side in the Vietnam War of the 50s, as well as in the American Vietnam War 1965-73. The US employed pilots from Air America for bomb missions against the "neutral" countries Laos and Cambodia, used by North Vietnam as a transit and base area; a grey area war indeed. The pilots were paid out of CIA secret funds.

When this took place, however, Chennnault was long dead for he passed away in 1958. He was a somewhat adventurous character, a mercenary-type general leading a soldier-of-fortune air force in the form of the AVG and other China Forces. He had "general talent"— he could deal with politicians and superior HQs as well as lead operations—but he overestimated the power of air forces in winning a war like the Chinese Civil War.

14. JAMES H. DOOLITTLE (1896-1993)

IN TANGIBLE TERMS, THE DOOLITTLE RAID did little damage. A few bombs were dropped on Tokyo and other cities and it wasn't the question of "cainitic destruction" – but – *psychologically* it was a shock to the Japanese, seeing bombers out of thin air harassing the land of Amaterasu, the sun goddess. The raid was named after its operational commander, the Air Force Lieutenant Colonel *James Harold Doolittle*. And in addition to the psychological dimension, this operation is said to have had far-reaching effects: it likely contributed to the Japanese decision of recalling a fleet from the Indian Ocean, instead focusing on the Pacific again and thus leading to the Battle of Midway, which became the greatest naval defeat ever for Japan.

Let's take it from the beginning. It was the new year of 1942 and the Americans had no reason for joy. Because, their pacific navy was sunk at Pearl Harbor and their semi-colonial possession the Philippines was invaded by superior Japanese forces, the archipelago being impossible to relieve right now. The Japanese were about to occupy all of East Asia. So the situation was dire—but—the US still had its three aircraft carriers intact: Hornet, Enterprise and Yorktown. This gave an air force staff officer an idea, namely, to bomb Tokyo with B-25 Mitchell bombers having started from aircraft carriers, approximately 400 nautical miles from the Japanese coast. Having completed the task the aircraft would land in China, in Nationalist controlled area, to refuel. The crews would eventually reach India and thus be able to get back to the United States in one way or another.

The boldest in this bold plan was to let the land-based B-25s start from aircraft carriers. Was it even possible?

Air Force commander at the time was Henry Harley "Hap" Arnold. And he immediately appreciated the plan, and soon he even had presidential approval: FDR liked everything aerial, a handy weapon of war not involving the deployment of ground troops. The man who was to lead the operation was aviation hero Jimmy Doolittle and at the beginning of March 1942, he had recruited his crews. It was 140 men from the 17th Bombardment Group. All men volunteered for this and were soon gathered at the Eglin Field base in Pensacola, Florida. Doolittle gave a speech to his men, saying that the imminent operation was extremely dangerous, so if anyone wanted to back out now he was free to go. But, of course, no one wanted to pull out, they were all in.

It was about using the North American Mitchell B-25 bomber, a twin-engine, mid-wing bomber named after Billy Mitchell whose ideas can be said to have been the basis for the mission: that bombers could have strategic effect, that armadas of heavy bombers could win the war, a concept inspired by Italian author Guilo Douet's *Il dominio dell'aria*. Normally, the B-25 had a starting distance of 500 meters but now it had to take off already after *170 meters;* this succeeded by lowering the landing flaps and give full throttle. The crews also practiced night flying and low-altitude bombing. But no crew by this time knew that they were going to start from an aircraft carrier.

The aircraft was equipped with an extra 300 liter petrol tank at the top of the bomb room, as well as an additional 200 liter tank where the dorsal MG turret normally was located. In addition, the top-secret Norden bombsights were removed and replaced by simpler devices, should any plane be captured by the Japanese. For the record, the planes had a system preventing icing of the wings' leading edges, channelizing waste heat from the engine cooling system through rubber ducts. But this may have been a standard feature of this aircraft type.

Everything was secret: Doolittle, for his part, went back and forth to Washington during the training program, he must travel by train to collect his orders in fear of the phones being tapped. In Washington, he also arranged the reception in China; Japan possessed it since 1937, primarily the coastal regions, so here and there in the hinterland Chiang's nationalists, who were US allies, ruled. The plan was that after the bombing of Tokyo the B-25s would land in the Nationalist controlled area; several small fields were booked for this stopover, fields where the planes would be refueled and then fly on to Chungking, Nationalist China's capital. Once there the crews would be considered safe since the USA had an air base in this town for the shipping of supplies from India to China. From Chungking, they would fly to India and from there through Africa to make it home to the States. As it would turn out no B-25 made its escape this way, flying under its own power to reach India; either the planes went down, were captured or were detained. More on the specific fates of the planes later.

On 25 March the unit was rebased to McClellan field in Sacramento, California. After further training it flew to Alameda in the San Francisco Bay where the crews got sight of the aircraft carrier USS Hornet lying at anchor – and then they began to understand the nature of their training, like, for instance, having short take-off distances. The sixteen planes landed and were taken aboard the ship; they must be kept on deck, occupying half of the deck space.

The next day, 1 April, the ship was out to sea. Now the crews were told that they would bomb Japan: Tokyo, Yokohama, Osaka, Kobe and Nagoya, strategically important cities. They also learned that after the bombing they would steer towards the south-west to eventually land on certain Chinese fields for refueling and further flight to Chungking in Sichuan. The planes would be loaded with three 250 kg bombs and a firebomb; naïvely it was believed that Tokyo would be up in flames if only seven of these firebombs hit because of the town having so many rice paper houses, but the reality was another, the effect of the firebombs was not at all as expected. Generally, the crews were ordered to bomb aircraft factories, iron works, and oil supplies – but not the imperial palace in Tokyo, this was holy ground. For its part, the crew of each plan was pilot, co-pilot, navigator, bombardier and aft MG gunner. Each airman got as special equipment a gun caliber .45, a hunting knife, supplies, and morphine.

At dawn on 18 April, when Hornet was 800 nautical miles from Japan, it was sighted by a Japanese patrol boat. The enemy vessel was quickly sunk by Hornet's escort destroyer but this still affected the bomb mission – because, now the risk was that the patrol boat had enough time to report back on the hostile carrier, so it was decided to start immediately. The original plan was to start in the afternoon of 19 April, flying over the towns and bomb them in the dark, flying through the night and land in China at dawn; now, however, the planes must fly an additional 400 nautical miles so each plane was given five extra 25 liter cans.

It was a great gamble and with the Japanese patrol boat appearing everything had become even more difficult, but of course, it had to be launched nonetheless. It was time to start and the first in line was Doolittle's plane. He revved up the engines, released the brakes and set off along the deck with an especially painted line as guidance – and precisely when Hornet, going full steam, was on the top of a wave the plane took off. It was heavily laden and had only a few meters to spare to the sea surface but Doolittle had the stick at maximum pull-back and eventually had the B-25 rise, people on the deck seeing the machine "virtually hanging by the propellers". Having gained height Doolittle made a turn, circled a few times and continued in the ship's direction – for Halsey, the ship's commander, as an orientation aid had set the ship on course to Tokyo. All the planes started happily and now it was just about forgetting formation flight since the start been so hasty; the planes flew west, *every plane for itself*. In a typical mission, the planes went up and circled a while until all had gathered, flying in formation towards the target as *an invincible armada* in the spirit of Guilio Douet.

Over the Pacific Ocean expanses the machines flew, green painted and with the old USAAF-marking on wings and fuselage, the one with a white star on a blue circle and a red dot in the center; later this variety was abandoned because the red dot tended to be confused with the Japanese *Hin-no-Maru*-mark, "the ascending sun." For his part, Doolittle flew as low as he could, about seven meters above the surface of the water. The cruising speed was relatively low. 1.30 p.m., after approximately five hours of flight, the Japanese coast was seen – and with some navigation, and following successive valleys, the correct valley was found, leading to Tokyo. It is said that Doolittle arrived over Tokyo in a psychologically interesting moment, at the very time when a radio broadcast in English assured the listeners that Tokyo would never be bombed. In his low-altitude approach to target, Doolittle, for instance, flew over a sports field where a baseball game was in progress and seeing the enemy planes in the sky the game was interrupted. Regarding this sport, baseball, the Japanese had been enthusiastic baseball players since the beginning of the century when the sport was introduced by the Americans. Doolittle eventually dropped his bombs, including the firebomb, over plants and storage buildings. On the way out, he flew straight over a field full of training planes and he loudly regretted that he didn't have any more bombs to drop.

When he flew in over the Chinese coast there was a storm but he flew over it. At ten in the evening, over friendly territory, the crew abandoned the plane by parachute jumping. The next day, after having been sleeping in a roadside ditch with the parachute as cover, Doolittle began walking and came to a village – and, in this village, he was told that if he had chosen a slightly different path he would have fallen into the hands of a Japanese patrol. Later Doolittle found his crashed plane in a rice paddy. With the help of the nationalist Chinese Doolittle and his crew, all of which landed happily after their jumps, soon reached Chungking for further transport to the USA.

Even the other planes of the unit had reached their targets and bombed them, and then heading for China (with one exception, see below). As for the crews, some survived and among the survivors, some ended up in captivity and could be released only after the end of the war. A short rhapsody of the crews' *diaspora* will tell us that one plane steered to Vladivostok in Soviet Russia where the airmen became detainees since Soviet and Japan were neutral among themselves. The rest of the planes were lost in China. The total number of crew members of the unit were originally eighty, and of these eleven died or were captured, and three of the eleven died after parachute jumping over China, and the remaining eight of the eleven were captured by the Japanese in China – and of these eight, three were executed while one died in captivity, probably through disease. Four men survived the captivity and were released in August 1945. The rest, the 69 airmen who neither died nor were captured, ended up with the Nationalist Chinese and could continue west via Chungking and India. Finally, no plane was shut down during the raid which says something about the surprise effect; no one crashed over Japan but all reached China, except for the one flying to Soviet.

Next, regarding the consequences of the raid. We have already intimated that the tangible results would be limited, no major damage was effected by the planes on the cities they bombed; at most, the effect was psychological. Neither did any serious *fires* occur, it would take the B-29 raids from Saipan in the spring of 1945 before Tokyo went up in flames. The effect was psychological. By this time the Japanese believed that they were unbeatable, the whole of south-east Asia having been conquered without any significant losses, and then, suddenly, they saw American bomber above their cities. This led to a redirection of the forces against the Americans whom the Japanese thought were completely knocked out after Pearl Harbor. Just how the B-25s had flown to their island the Japanese didn't quite understand—but—they now began to make plans to crush the remaining US fleet in the Pacific, plans being drawn up for what would become the *Battle of Midway*. This was fought 4-6 June 1942 and came to be Japan's first naval defeat in modern times, losing four aircraft carriers while the Americans only lost one. So if Midway was a turning point battle, which is usually maintained, we can say that the Doolittle raid contributed to turning the war.

Finally, a few words about the man who led the operation, Jimmy Doolittle himself. He was born in 1896, was during WWI army pilot and instructor and became Second Lieutenant in 1920. He received a PhD in physics in 1925 at MIT. He took his leave of the air force in 1930. Now he started working for the flight department of the Shell Oil company and flew racing aircraft. The unofficial world record for 1932 was held by Doolittle in the plane *Gee-Bee Super Sportster,* flying at 471 km/h.

In WWII Doolittle returned to active service. The Tokyo raid rendered him the United States' supreme decoration, the Congressional Medal of Honor. Having been promoted Major General he led operations in Europe, North Africa, and the Pacific. After the war, he worked as a consultant for Shell. He retired in 1959 and died very old, at 96 years of age in September 1993.

15. LESLIE R. GROVES (1896-1970)

THE SUBJECT OF "THE CAPITAL cities of the American states" is a thing of itself. As for non-Americans, how many, for example, know that California's capital neither is Los Angeles nor San Francisco, but Sacramento? Or that the Florida capital city isn't Miami but Tallahassee? Or that the state of New York's capital city isn't New York but Albany? In any case, in this Albany was born a certain *Leslie Richard Groves* in 1896, as the son of a military chaplain.

Leslie Groves studied at MIT and attended the abbreviated West Point course during WWI. He graduated as number four—but— now it was already 1918 and Groves didn't have the time to see any of the war. He was inter alia posted in Nicaragua and in Hawaii and soon ended up in the *Engineer Corps,* the army unit for buildings, fortifications, and fixed installations. During the early stage of WWII Groves was given charge of the construction of the *Pentagon,* a single headquarters in Washington for the navy and the army; so far, the diverse HQ facilities had been scattered over many different places in the capital city, but the escalation to total war had increased the armed forces' need for administrative buildings. Of the Pentagon can also be said that it is a five-sided complex with concentrically arranged rows of buildings. In the middle is a courtyard used for medal awarding ceremonies, welcoming of foreign dignitaries and so on. As it should be, the best office is the one of the Chairman of the Joint Chiefs of Staff, in the 1990s located on the second floor directly above the entrance, and not far from there the Defense Secretary has his office. In the American management model, the governmental departments are integrated with their subject ministries; it isn't like, say, in Sweden where we have a separate department of defense and a separate defense headquarters – for, in the US, both are merged in the Pentagon. Thus, the Secretary of Defense has his office in the Pentagon, too; he is the civilian leader of the Republic's defense in both war peace. How much influence he had in reality was a difficult situation, of course, depending on the people surrounding him – in short, depending on who is the president, who is CJCS and (to some extent) who commands the field armies.

It is said that at first, they planned to build the Pentagon completely without windows. The whole structure would be one, single large bunker protected from aerial attack. From the aesthetic point of view, it was fortunate that this plan was never realized for such a five-sided sarcophagus would have made a "titanic, cyclopean" impression.

Leslie Groves belonged to the Engineer Corps. He wasn't a combat engineer proper—but—in order to delve on that function, the field army engineers, it can be said that they build roads, bridges, and fortifications and they can also destroy them, they can lay out mines and clear mines and much more. Theirs is a supporting role, not primarily a combat role. In this context, the fighting is done by infantry, armor, and to a certain extent artillery (artillery, too is support but it does a lot to win the battles). Then there is the leading element in the form of staffs, HQs and signal troops. And these three elements are what all armies consist of, *leading, fighting,* and *supporting,* and, if you like, this is a reflection of the medieval class society of priests, warriors, and workers, *oratores, bellatores,* and *laboratores,* equal to the ancient Indian *brahmanas, kshatriyas,* and *vaishyas.* In the US Army of the nineteenth century, this would be formalized by having a leadership of *Commanding, Adjutant,* and *Quarter Master General,* that is, an army commander, a chief of staff, and a logistics manager. This came after the Civil War. The Commanding General would gather up the reins and lead the armies, the Adjutant General would assist with plans and intelligence and the Quarter Master General would arrange the maintenance.

Dedicated maintenance and engineering troops arrived in the nineteenth century. Regarding engineers, of course, there had been army woodworkers and sappers before, steady men in beard and aprons building fortifications and obstacles, but the French-Austrian war in the 1850s made the *need for troops who could quickly build bridges* obvious. Thus, special engineer troops were born.

When we now are looking at the phenomenon of *army maintenance*, this is a fine moment to make an overview of US army material in the middle of the 20th century; as such, of course not exhaustive but giving you some insights into the WWII symbolical reality, American style. Regarding, for example, the food, there were a number of different preserves, in rather attractive packages having acquired an almost mythical role. Those having seen the Swedish army chocolate bar, 80 g, in the grey-brown paper, know what I'm talking about.

First, among the US preserves of the era, there was the *K Ration,* consisting of a can of a mixture of ham, cheese, and eggs or minced meat, a chocolate bar, four cigarettes, and a coffee or juice concentrate. For its part, *C Ration* was less luxurious and consisted of hotchpotch with sausage or macaroni while *D Ration* only consisted of a dark chocolate bar mixed with egg white. The most famous of these three was, of course, the K Ration, meant to sustain a man for 24 hours or so if cut off from the ration team. It was wrapped in a bluish paper; when the US occupied Japan children collected the discarded paper in the belief that it was something valuable, as indeed it was, it was useless and therefore invaluable.

We now turn to the weapons side of things. An important weapon was *the machine gun* where you can begin by mentioning *Browning M-1919,* arriving this year (1919) and being a light MG in caliber 7.62 mm. In inches, this will be 0.30. It occurred in infantry companies as well as vehicle armament, a common piece in WWII but today long out of use. Then there was the heavy *Browning M-2* in 12.7 mm caliber (.50), used as additional armament on combat vehicles, as an AA MG and as aircraft armament on fighters and bombers. Regarding its look, the most typical feature was the two vertical handles at the rear.

Concerning *sub-machine guns* we both have the *Thompson* from 1928, with the rather substantial caliber of 11.4 mm (.45), having either a drum magazine with fifty cartridges or with a straight magazine with twenty; the weapon was used in the gangster wars in Chicago in the 20s and was then given the nickname "Chicago Typewriter." A simpler and lighter sub-machine gun that was produced during WWII, with the outer casing made of pressed sheet steel and entirely without Thompson's wooden craftsmanship, was *M-3*, also known as "Grease Gun" because it looked like such an instrument, a grease gun used for lubrication of vehicles and such. It was caliber 11.4 mm, had a magazine with 30 rounds and weighed 3.7 kg, compared to Thompsons 4.9.

The American standard rifle during WWII was *Garand M-1* with a caliber of 7.62. It was a semi-automatic weapon: gunpowder gases from the fired cartridge brought a new cartridge into the chamber while simultaneously pressing the bolt back, but the trigger must be pulled again for each new shot. It was the world's first semi-automatic rifle adopted as the standard weapons in an army, decided on in the 1930s when MacArthur was Army Chief of Staff. M-1 had eight rounds in the magazine, fully integrated into the gunstock. It was produced in 5.5 million copies by the factories Springfield and Winchester. More copies, however, were made of the *M-1 carbine,* launched in 1941 and with a 7.62 mm pistol cartridge, rimless in contrast to the Garand cartridge. It was meant as a lighter weapon for drivers, artillerymen and such; this semi-automatic weapon is said to have been obsolete when it came out since the fully automatic, recoil driven M-3 had been adopted by this time. Also, it looked a bit old-fashioned with its gunstock made of wood, even if a variety with folding stock in the form of a bent steel bar arrived later, as used by paratroopers.

Regarding *pistols and revolvers,* US Army still during the WWII used revolvers of the Wild West-type, like the Colt Army from 1873 of caliber .45 and a rotating drum magazine of six shots. A modern pistol, however, had already arrived in 1911 from the same company (Colt), with the magazine for the .45 projectiles integrated into the butt and with automatic reloading, that is, an *automatic pistol.*

The last infantry weapon we will mention in this exposition will be the rocket launcher *Bazooka,* a 60 mm recoilless antitank weapon according to the principle of "free blowback," the free ejection of gunpowder gas through the open backend. Electric ignition fired rocket-propelled projectiles that could pierce 12.7 cm armor at a distance of 100-300 meters. This was a technical revolution, a first-generation lightweight portable anti-tank weapon. Until then, you had to have heavy artillery pieces to successfully combat armor, heavy ordnance which must be drawn by vehicles and be served by several men. However, the famed Bazooka had its disadvantages, like the gases emanating from the fired projectile which the shooter must be protected from, and in the flame striking out behind the weapon which made it easy to detect. It is said that the Germans laid their hands on a copy of this weapon in 1942, used by the Russians who received them as American aid, and with this model, the Germans designed the *Panzerbüchse* or *Panzerschreck* which was a similar antitank arm but with 88 mm caliber.

More weapons there were indeed in the US Army such as grenade launchers and artillery but those we will pass by here – while, of course, formally remembering the fundamental role of artillery in WWII in Patton's words: "I do not have to tell you who won the war. You know the artillery did." Instead, we will look at some *tanks.* The most important American tank in the war was *Sherman,* which was actually too small when for example meeting the Germans' heaviest models—but—there was a method in the madness. The Sherman was an all-round tank, one that could be used in both Europe and the Pacific Theater of Operations, and capable to stow into a landing craft in amphibious operations. This is why the vehicle had its relatively limited external dimensions. When the Sherman, then, for example, met a Tiger tank in Europe it had to readjust its tactics accordingly, like withdrawing and sneaking up on the Tiger's flanks to get a shorter range of fire. Furthermore, there was the *Grant tank,* equipped with one piece in a rotating tower and a heavier piece in the chassis, variable only a few degrees in the lateral direction. A third tank was *M-24*

Chaffee, a light tank named after the American armor theoretician, Adna Chaffee.

Regarding the soldier's personal equipment it may be sufficient to mention the *cigarette lighter* that has become a classic, the *Zippo lighter* which was made after the specification that it would light up even in a storm. It was a petrol refillable lighter where the liquid was sucked up by a kind of sponge, linked to a wick which was lit with a rifled wheel drawing sparks from a piece of flint. When worn down the flints could be replaced. In general, the American soldier's *t-shirts, chinos, fatigues* et cetera were stamped with the letters "G. I.," *Government Issue,* "state property," from which we have the nickname "G. I. Joe" for the American soldier. Towards the end of the war, the standard uniform issue was of a kind of cotton cloth greyish green in color, *olive drab,* while the Marine Corps had camouflage uniforms.

***

Back to Groves. It was his experience in carrying out major construction projects, like the Pentagon, that made Marshall appoint him as the *Manhattan Project* logistics manager; scientific manager was Robert Oppenheimer, the nuclear physicist. The Manhattan Project had been launched to produce a nuclear bomb and Groves was recruited in the summer of 1942. Until then an admiral had led it, a man not making things happen fast enough, but with Groves at the helm, there was a faster pace. This is illustrated by, for example, the fact that at the first meeting the army leadership had with Groves as project manager he excused himself halfway into this, saying that he must travel to a certain place to arrange a certain thing for the project. This left a great impression on the others; they had found their man. Groves' task was to recruit scientists and monitor the atomic research and build laboratories and factories of gigantic dimensions. It was primarily about creating the facility in Los Alamos in the south-west of the United States; from nothing would be built a city of 150,000 people in the desert wilderness.

The Manhattan Project was completed in August 1945 with the dropping of two nuclear bombs over Japan. During the project, Groves was never more than a colonel, however, temporarily he was promoted to Brigadier, that is, *brevet Brigadier,* having the prerogatives of the rank without its pay, as such a rather common practice in war. In 1948 Leslie Groves resigned from the army and became head of the research department at Remington Rand, the same company that a certain MacArthur was employed by after his retirement. Groves died in 1970.

16. CHARLES YEAGER (1923-)

W E WOULD LIKE TO SAY that *Charles Elwood "Chuck" Yeager* was courageous. Details aside, he represents *courage* in his roles as a fighter pilot, test pilot, and breaker of the sound barrier, a man being able to fly almost any plane after only brief instructions. The pinnacles of his career deserve some awe. You can't just relativize it and say that "he was merely the right man in the right place, if he hadn't done it someone else would have done it"—which, for its part, is an attitude ending up in a grey no man's land where there is no bravery, no responsibility, no creativity, no zest, no pizazz, no glory—nothing.

Yeager was born in 1923 in West Virginia as a *hillbilly;* he uses the term himself in his memoirs, belonging to a stock of poor white mountain-dwelling people. But it was a happy childhood with time off spent in the woods, like hunting and fishing. In 1941 he enlisted in the air force. He started as a mechanic and became a pilot because of an opportunity that presented itself. It quickly became clear that he had an inborn talent for flying.

WWII was raging by this time and the pilot cadets were taught the basics in the plane Bell P-39, a single-seat fighter with nose wheel and the engine behind the cockpit; disliked by combat pilots it had been reduced to the role of trainer aircraft. Yeager for his part liked the plane but he knew the chant (technically a limerick):

Don't give me a P-39

with an engine that's mounted behind.

It'll tumble and roll,

and dig a big hole –

don't give me a P-39.

When the training was completed Yeager was stationed in England as Mustang pilot with the 9th Tactical Air Command. The year was 1944 and the task was to escort bombers on raids over Germany, and thanks to the Mustang the fighter squadrons now could follow the bombers quite a long way – for previously, when only Spitfires were available, the fighter escorts had to leave and return home when reaching the German border because of shorter range for this aircraft type. The Mustang, however, had drop tanks assuring a longer range – and it had four to six machine guns and a sleek design, a fine example of "what looks good usually is good". Another American landmark plane now putting its mark on history was the Thunderbolt, a more ungainly design but this single-engine fighter was better than the Mustang in the attack and ground support role. For instance, in the battle environment, the radial engine of the Thunderbolt could sustain machine gun fire better than the Mustang inline engine.

Yeager's WWII service over Europe was dramatic but we'll bypass it here and move on to his post-war career, which began no less dramatically with him being a test pilot for the air force. It was an interesting time with jet planes coming of age and the implicit approaching of the mystic sound barrier – the very barrier that Yeager would be the first in the world to break through. It would be done in 1947 in the *Bell X-1*, a rocket plane designated for this.

The speed of sound is approximately 1,000 km/h (Mach 1). Already when reaching 800 km/h, for example with a piston engine aircraft in a dive, it was noticed how the plane started shaking and how the controls seemingly "froze," they got stuck. This was due to pressure waves being formed at the speed of sound, shock waves hitting rudder and stabilizer making the plane uncontrollable; many had crashed in these circumstances. For example, the Brits at the time were flying their tailless de Havilland DH 108 very close to "sound barrier velocities"—but—the three extant DH 108 prototypes eventually crashed, one after the other. Due to it having no tail, like a Me 163...? Due to the magical qualities of "the sound barrier"...?

The signs were ominous. It was thought by some that the sound barrier was very tangible, a solid wall that all planes slammed into when they approached 1,000 km/h.

The American company Bell tried to approach the problem of supersonic speed with the system Bell X-1, a rocket plane carried by a B-29 bomber taking it up to cruise altitude, 7,500 meters. When released from the mother ship, the X-1 pilot would ignite the plane's four rockets and attempt at Mach 1 in a climb, not a dive. Also, the whole stabilizer could be tilted, operated with a servo, avoiding the controls to be stuck when the pressure waves hit.

This, with Yeager at the controls, did it. It took many flights, many briefings and de-briefings to get to the heart of the problem (like actually using the tilting stabilizer), but they did it. "The best men will have the best machines" as Jünger once said. It was state-of-the-art technology and timeless bravery in cooperation; like, at one stage in the program Yeager had the feeling that he really *would* make it, that the sound barrier was a myth, and this "willpower-and-vision of the hero" is crucial to get things done in this world. This is material in writing history. You can't sit in a lab (or an HQ, or a café) and plan success – no, you have to "get up and go" too, tangibly test the system in real life.

Yeager's historical Mach 1 flight (actually Mach 1.07 – 1,126 km/h), the breaking of the sound barrier, was done at Muroc Air Force Base in California, on 14 October 1947.

As for Yeager, he stayed on for some years as a test pilot at Muroc, subsequently renamed Edwards, flying rocket planes and prototype jet aircraft, designs benefiting from the research data gained by the X-1 flight. For instance, he tested what would become the *Century series,* planes like F-100 Super Sabre, F-104 Starfighter and so on, titanium shimmering symbols of the jet age. F stands for "fighter" and as a fighter pilot, Yeager belonged to the US Air Force Tactical Command; there were also bombers in the Strategic Air Command and air defense of the US mainland in the Air National Guard. Next, after being a test pilot Yeager had to serve in the Air Force "cold war front line" for a while, being appointed squadron commander of a fighter group, based in Germany; it had planes of the type F-86 Sabre. An event worthy of note is the Hungary Crisis of 1956 when all NATO airbases were on alert; Yeager's group even loaded small atomic bombs on their planes and were prepared to fly towards the Soviet Union to bomb it if necessary. But the alert was called off and Yeager was glad of this, for instance, because of not having to go bomb Moscow and thus not having to walk back, the range of the F-86 being rather limited for missions like these. "Being forced to go home by foot when you've dropped an atomic bomb" may sound irrelevant but it is details like these people can relate to, while a thing like *dropping an atomic bomb over the enemy* is difficult to really imagine.

In the mid-60s Yeager was commander of the air force astronaut school in the X-15-project, based at Edwards. This was a further development of X-1 the and other experimental planes of the 50s, this one intended as a spaceship that could land aerodynamically and not as a space capsule virtually falling right down after launch and orbit. The X-15 project was subsequently wound down precisely in favor of "capsules and rockets" but it did contribute to the later concept of the Space Shuttle. And the X-15 itself really did go out into space, like in 1963 reaching the altitude of 107,000 meters, the legal limit for space being 100,000 meters. The X-15 would be taken up to normal flight altitude by being carried under the belly of a B-52; then it was released, switching on its rocket engines, striving for 80-100,000 meter altitude and then glide down. Yeager never flew this plane, he technically never was out in space but he did make one attempt at an altitude record in an F-104 Starfighter used at this astronaut flight school, the aircraft being equipped with an extra rocket engine at the rear enabling the ship to reach 30,000 meter altitude, a height were the laws of aerodynamics stopped being applicable and you had to have special nozzles with hydrogen peroxide mounted on the plane to operate it. Thus equipped the plane roughly reminded you of an X-15 which was the whole point, the astronauts getting used to near-space properties flying it.

One day in 1963 Yeager got the urge to set a new altitude record for aircraft having started by its own engine. The Russians had the current record, 38,160 meters – and Yeager took the specially treated F-104 and got going. In the film *The Right Stuff* (1983) this is well rendered, a last heroic feat, a "final shot at glory" by Yeager to end the movie, the drama having begun with his X-1 flight in 1947 and having the Mercury space program in between. Yeager also, of course, tells of this altitude record attempt in his memoirs—and, there we read that he took the plane up to 10,000 meters with ordinary jet engine power—and then switching on the booster rocket to strive for 30,000. However, in this critical phase, he began to lose control, having neither the power to go further up nor the power to pitch down the nose to get a better angle of attack, this "pitching down" to be done with the peroxide nozzles. Because the air around was still too dense for the trustors to have any effect, they only worked in vacuum or near-vacuum. And the ordinary rudder and stabilizer didn't work in this thin air. So he lost control of the plane and went into a spin, being finally forced to emergency eject by the catapult seat, gliding by parachute to the ground.

Details aside it was a dangerous ascent, like Yeager when free of the plane being hit by the ejected seat itself and, also, having difficulties to breathe. All told a heroic feat.

As for the purpose of pitching down the nose, it was intended at reducing the pitch angle just a little and then continue the ascent to 38,000 m and higher to beat the record. The problem with the weak nozzles began at 32,000 m altitude.

Yeager also had a tour of duty in Vietnam, for instance flying fighter-bombers and lecturing the pilots on how to do it. By this time he became Brigadier General, a rank he also had when he retired. He admits that he was a good pilot while also not so versed in the theoretical side of flying. The latter, however, is needed when being a test pilot—but—when Yeager was flying the X-1 he had one fine engineer ally, breaking down the facts and figures for him. Otherwise, Yeager had a fine technical instinct bordering on intuition.

We shall end this chapter with a few anecdotes from the memoirs – *Yeager*.

Pro primo. When jet planes came of age Yeager went around demonstrating this new phenomenon to the public, flying a P-80 Shooting Star. He would then fool people that the plane was started like a blow torch, having to put something like a burning newspaper behind the exhaust. Someone in the audience was asked to do this, light a newspaper and hold it behind the plane, and then Yeager would sit in the cockpit and start it the usual, correct manner by switching on the engine, which no one saw.

Pro secondo. When Yeager was test pilot, his wife was so accustomed to him risking his life on the job flying jet prototypes, that when he one day came home pale and sweaty after work she thought that he had been in a car accident. She didn't connect it to the flying activity but this time it was a near run thing, he had been close to crashing in an X-1 A rocket plane.

Pro tertio. Yeager was familiar with Jackie Cochran, a female record-holding pilot married to a millionaire. When her husband died, his last wish was to have his ashes scattered over the large property he had. Yeager and a pilot buddy decided to spread the ash by aircraft. Said and done and up in the air, where one was at the control and the other spread the dust through an open door – but then it was noticed that this was no good method, half of the ashes blew back into the plane because of backwash...

17. THE KOREAN WAR

THE KOREAN WAR WAS A semi-colonial war waged beyond the seas. However, in the short term, the US in this conflict defended territory it had acquired at the end of WWII so to defend yourself against the communist attack was rather natural. There was operationally never any doubt about what should be done when the communists attacked at dawn on 25 June 1950.

It began by North Korean forces crossing the 38th parallel, the border of the Republic of Korea ("South Korea"). The force was no less than seven infantry divisions and one armored division with the most modern variant of T-34 tanks, supplied by Russia. At the same time, the North Korean air force hit targets around the capital of South Korea, Seoul, located just south of the border. The city was taken on 28 June and at the beginning of July, the North Korean armored spearhead had reached halfway down the length of South Korea, the southern part of the Korean peninsula. North Korea, the region and subsequent communist state "liberated" by the Soviet at the end of the war, was situated north of this, between South Korea and the Chinese province of Manchuria. The two Koreas were separated by a provisional line, a demarcation line roughly along the 38th parallel. At the time of writing this line still separates the two states, like a Berlin wall of the east.

But what did the United States do in the meantime, in 1950? The US troops occupying South Korea wasn't much to put up against the aggression. But as soon as the news of the attack arrived President Truman decided to act, to defend the southern Korean realm. Preliminarily, four US divisions were shipped from Japan to South

Korea, 8th Army troops being this way brought out of their lethargy, its soldiers being poorly trained and mentally unprepared to fight a war. In the aftermath of WWII, no one really believed in a war erupting. Next, the USA obtained a UN resolution which called on the members to stop the aggression in Korea; many countries contributed with various military units but the main part of the forces was supplied by the Americans. (In the following the "Western" side of the contestants will be called things like "the UN troops, the Allies, the Americans". The other side: "the Communists".)

On 8 July MacArthur, leader of the American occupation of Japan, was appointed UN military commander in Korea.

The four US divisions sent to Korea deployed not so far from the demarcation line, but they had to retreat in the initial battles. Among other things, it had problems to knock out the T-34 tanks of the enemy, as in the battle of 5 July at Osan, somewhere south of Seoul. 75 mm M20 recoilless grenades and bazooka projectiles were nothing against this armor; it was only when armor piercing 105 mm artillery hit the column that two vehicles were knocked out. Generally, it was about retreating here and elsewhere, the UN force soon deploying in a strong defensive deployment at the southern tip of the peninsula with Pusan as a port. The commander of 8th Army, *Walton Walker* (1889-1950), a short, blunt fellow, had previously served under Patton. In the ensuing battle, he was able to defend the bridgehead. UN aerial units at the same time attacked the Communist supply lines. Soon the crisis was over, the Pusan bridgehead withstood the attacks and supplies could continue to be shipped over from Japan. But these had been hard days, symbolized in this order of Walker to one of his subordinates: *I'm sending you up the river to die...*

At the same time, larger things were in the pipeline. Just like the Italian peninsula during WWII Korea was suitable for amphibious landings, surprising flank attacks. The Italian lesson was that the defender could contain such "surprising" attacks (Anzio). However, here in Korea, the method was a success. It was the landing at Inchon, Seoul's port city on the west coast. On 15 September this was the place of landing two divisions from the Marines which surprised the enemy, the Communists soon abandoning Inchon at the same time as Walker broke out from Pusan. The whole strategic situation was changed in an instant, the Allies soon being able to retake Seoul, and then reaching the starting point, the 38th parallel. For its part, the Inchon landings could remind you of MacArthur's Pacific War days, an amphibious operation executed in a surprising direction. But, those in the know also knew that Mac was capable of such feats, this was *Common Knowledge* which also was the name of this 1950 operation.

With this victory under the belt, the UN General Assembly adopted a new resolution: the whole of Korea would now be liberated. And soon the UN troops with Americans in the lead invaded North Korea, with victory in sight heading for the Chinese border. Some feared that China would intervene, whereof signals certainly arrived, sent by the Chinese themselves through diplomatic channels – but the Allies chose to ignore this and MacArthur himself assuredly said that there was no risk. The North Korean capital Pyongyang was taken. In October 1950, this enabled the production and sending of an episode of "The Bob Hope Show," announced as the first TV program recorded in a liberated communist city... Once at the Yalu River, the Chinese border area being reached in the late autumn of 1950, most of the troops believed that the war was virtually over. Among other things surplus ammunition was sent back – for this, they would surely not need...?

However, they would need it. On 26 November two Chinese armies attacked over the Yalu River, a total surprise for MacArthur and many others. Strategically, this was yet another example of *how wishful thinking can deceive a general,* this way of assuming the enemy will act in such a way that you expect him to do. Custer was led astray this way at Little Bighorn, and Bradley and Hodges in the Ardennes in December 1944. *One* subtle reason for the current setback may have been that the United States still believed itself to have some goodwill on the part of the Chinese, the people they seemingly had done so much for in WWII with the support to Chiang, the Flying Tigers and all that. Perhaps the US was also completely unaware that Mao's China was the main supporter of North Korea in the ongoing war, perhaps it ignored this fact, for with a better grasp of the general situation the Americans would surely not have advanced towards the Yalu in such a casual manner.

As a comparison: if a superpower army advanced upon the US-Mexican border, would the US be able to ignore it?

In any event, the Americans were surprised and were forced to make a quick retreat. Overall, the physical condition of many soldiers was poor; many soldiers just straggled behind and were taken prisoner by the Communists. The Allies could generally retreat with the maintained cohesion of units, no large encirclements were made, but morally this was a stinging defeat for the United States, being beaten by soldiers of a third world army in this way. US Army was well equipped with combat vehicles and trucks while the Chinese mostly went by foot. And as for small unit communications, the Americans had walkie-talkies while the Chinese had *trumpets* in the old style: it worked well, we can tell you. And the US had all its formidable *air support,* both from ground bases and from aircraft carriers – but still, it had to give ground.

The Allies retreated to the 38th parallel. The United Nations Alliance leaders sat down to deliberate. It was recognized that they had to stay put, deploy for defense, maybe settle for a draw. But MacArthur for his part protested, he wanted to bring the war to a victorious end: "There is no substitute for victory," he said. And, to a journalist asking if that could be done with the use of atomic weapons, he said that this couldn't be ruled out. Thus, to the public Mac seemed to be out of touch with reality, he had grown too large for his role and he was officially dismissed, for you cannot have such a willful general in the field. Truman sacked him and he did the right thing, even if some people at the time stood in awe before MacArthur's greatness and thought that Truman had made a serious mistake. This was in April 1951.

The replacement for Mac was *Matthew Ridgway.* In WWII he had commanded parachute operations, from Sicily 1943 to

Normandy and Arnhem 1944. When Walton Walker died in a jeep accident in Korea, December 1950, Ridgway succeeded him as 8th Army Commander. The 1951 succession took place in a difficult situation, during the retreat from Yalu, but Ridgway managed to restore morale in a short period of time. Regarding the image, for his part, Walker had been something of a cowboy while Ridgway gave a more restrained impression: he was always dressed in full field equipment with helmet and canvas webbing, and on each shoulder strap wearing a grenade and a first-aid kit. The soldier's humor turned this into two grenades and gave him the nickname "Old Iron Tits"...

As Commander-in-Chief in Korea Ridgway now introduced some changes. Until then the soldiers didn't really know what they fought for, but now they were told that the holding back of China was necessary for the national security. However, this wouldn't mean transferring the war onto Chinese territory, that would be too costly; the other commitments of the US, especially in Europe, would suffer. Ridgway also changed the tactics of the ground troops. Previously they had tended to hang on to their vehicles, amassing on the roads, but now the general order was to deploy in the terrain; Ridgway was an old paratrooper and in this way had the troops behave in a more "ranger-like" fashion. As for the fighting, it was now confined to the 38th parallel, a US defensive succeeding in containing major Communist breakthroughs. The enemy side was ground down and suffered rather heavy losses.

In 1952 Ridgway was succeeded by *Mark Clark*, having previously been head of the American 5th Army in Italy 1943-45. As intimated Italy reminds you of Korea as the elongated peninsula it is, and the terrain itself is rather similar with substantial mountains and little room for maneuver, troop movements being channelized in the valley gorges. As Korea C-in-C, Clark suggested the use of atomic weapons in order to break the deadlock, but unlike MacArthur, he didn't put himself on a collision course with Pentagon and President. The battles continued along the mainly stabilized front, and the United States, therefore, decided to transfer a part of the responsibility to Korean troops. The relationship between the Americans and the Koreans were not the best but at the signing of the cease-fire of 1953 two thirds of the front was held by the South Korean Army.

In July 1953, it was clear neither side could win, neither would be the master of a united Korea – so the country was divided into two parts along the 38th parallel, North and South Korea. Mark Clark said in his memoirs that he signed the cease-fire agreement with a heavy heart, having wanted to bring the war to a victorious conclusion but having to be content with a tie. He thus became the first American C-in-C not to win a war.

Comparing Korea to Vietnam it usually appears that the former war was fine and honest, inter alia because the operations were clear with distinct front lines, a war of offensives and retreats in the style of "large unit maneuver warfare". But at the same time, you shouldn't whitewash the Korean War. Take, for instance, American losses; they were 50,000 in Korea compared to 58,000 in Vietnam, so there is little difference. Further, the Korean civilian population was pretty much affected by the aerial bombing, the 50s US Air Force having a considerable strength and in Korea, air support was used as often as possible. It would suffice that a hostile sniper deployed in a village, stifling an advancing column, for the village in question to be wiped out by aerial bombing. It is said that relatively, Korea was hit harder by air bombing than Japan during WWII, which is rather appalling.

18. THE VIETNAM WAR

IETNAM IS A COUNTRY TO THE south of China. In the nineteenth century, it was a French colony. In 1940, the Japanese took over everything. A certain *Ho Chi-Minh* then formed the movement *Viet Minh* to put an end to all foreign involvement in Vietnam.

After WWII, in 1945, Ho in the north of the land, Tonkin, proclaimed his Democratic Republic of Vietnam, with the ambition to take over the whole country, the southern parts of Cochin China and Annam then held by Allied occupation forces. In WWII Ho had been an American ally, supported by them to fight the Japanese in the region. Since the Japanese in the final phase of the war had arrested all French lower officials of the administration, it was easy for Ho to take power. An interesting note on Ho during the war is this: he once visited general Chennault in one of his China stations, asking to have his signed photograph. Ho could later use this photo as a proof of having powerful allies, he was indeed friends with a US general. This anecdote also illustrates the prestige and goodwill the Americans enjoyed in Asia at the time.

In 1945 Ho Chi-Minh held the northern part of the country and the south was occupied by a British Army Division; in October this year the British handed over the region to the French, thus returning to its old colonial possession. The French Constitution of the year 1946 for its part said that the old colonies in Indochina would be part of a union with the mother country, France – and in March of the same year it recognized Ho Chi-Minh's Republic as a free state within the French Union, but further negotiations foundered. The French tried to take Tonkin by force of arms, but this failed after the Battle of Dien Bien Phu in 1954.

The French then abandoned all its east Asian colonies. But the Americans, having supported the French with arms during the war, now stepped in to support South Vietnam; a peace agreement concluded in Paris in 1954 namely partitioned the country into a southern and a northern part, across the waist of the province of Annam, with the ulterior motive that the two would soon be reunited after elections. But the mistrust was too large, the USA seeing North Vietnam which was supported by China as a new North Korea, so the elections in the south was stopped. The United States went in to fully support South Vietnam, a puppet regime held under the armpits with financial aid, done by for example sending it *military advisers*, something that the Paris Agreement allowed – but only to a number of 600. This figure the United States exceeded in secret so that by the autumn of 1963, there were no less than 17,000 (*seventeen thousand*) US military personnel in Vietnam.

North Vietnam worked to destabilize South Vietnam in various ways. There was a Communist aggression, Stanley Karnow states in his *Vietnam - A History*. The FNL—Front National de Libération —was a hostile, communist-led threat to South Vietnam, not a spontaneous popular rebellion. Thus, the US had some justification in saying that it helped South Vietnam to turn down the subversive activity of FNL by sending weapons and advisers.

The American advisers became involved in a guerrilla war with the FNL, although only intended to work as instructors often participating in combat. But the war was going badly and the FNL was completely in control of the Southern Vietnamese rural regions, an area where they moved as fish in the water according to Mao's guerrilla doctrine, dressed in farmer's black pajamas and bamboo hats. Politics aside, aggression aside, maybe these FNL fighters and Northern Vietnamese had more stamina, maybe they had a more warlike spirit, while the Southern Vietnamese were a bit more cultured and less inclined for the warrior's way. The North was hardened by war with China while the South was less shaped by this. Historically, the pattern of *a culturally advanced south against a more primitive and tougher north* can also be seen in circumstances like Mexico versus the USA, South versus North in the Civil War and China's rice-growing, bureaucrat-run southern region against the wheat-growing warrior states in the north. Regarding the Mexican higher culture, it was noted by Robert E. Lee when he campaigned there in the 1840s: it was a neat and prosperous rural land despite the formal poverty, Mexican villages giving a richer impression than corresponding American communities north of the border. It was a richer breeding ground here, having a more fertile cultural soil thanks to overlays in the form of different Indian cultures—Toltec, Maya, Aztec—than in the neighboring United States being mostly desert and steppe, uninhabited since the dawn of time except for the odd nomad tribe passing by. And regarding the high culture of the South during the Civil War it's widely known that the South had a richer literature and a more courteous manner between people. In the North it was a kind of "meat and potatoes, wearing the hat on indoors" – culture, for example in cities like New York.

Head of the American military mission in Vietnam at the time was *Paul Harkins* (1904-1984), a cavalry and a polo enthusiast. During WWII he had served in the headquarters of Patton's 3rd Army. In Vietnam, he was more of a sort of general diplomat than a Chief Operating Officer. Of the current Counter-Insurgency (COIN) war he had no idea. For example, during Harkin's reign, the counting of dead enemy bodies ("body count") began to be used a measure of success in fighting, which shows his unrealistic, bureaucratic attitude. Very illustrative of Harkin's nature is the anecdote of when he was asked to place himself among a group of soldiers for a press photo. He refused with the motivation, *I'm not that kind of general...*

The war was going badly and the guerrillas threatened to topple South Vietnam. By then, the United States wasn't involved in full scale. This changed in 1965 when the guerrillas attacked garrisons in Pleiku and Qui Nanh where 38 American advisers were killed and 100 wounded. President Johnson then gave the green light to air strikes on North Vietnam, done by planes from the aircraft carrier Ranger bombing two minor cities in the north. At the same time, regular troops were sent in, 2,000 Marines that would protect an airbase in Da Nang. Soon followed a series of army units and at the end of the year, 200,000 troops had been sent to Vietnam. All other things being equal, this was a time of increased focus on *armies*, on *ground forces*, these having been in the strategic doldrums since the end of WWII, the Korean War only temporarily putting its focus on them. Otherwise, aerial forces were hailed. But it was noticed that the balance of terror brought on by atomic weapons enabled the Communist bloc to advance globally, using guerrillas, a move impossible to stop with grand scale methods of war. Thus, counter-insurgency warfare (COIN) became a popular concept, stressing the need for highly trained special ground forces. With these (and regular Army/Marine Corps units) you could put down diverse "brushfire wars," was the idea.

Let us return to the sequence of events. For its part, air strikes toward the north were begun in February 1965 and lasted almost daily to 1968. They became a fiasco – for it was thought from the beginning that three weeks of bombing would bring the North Vietnamese to their knees, but not even three *years* of the bombing was enough, it would later prove. The USA launched this Operation Rolling Thunder with carrier-based aircraft, then added land-based aircraft like F-105 Thunderchief, and when that wasn't enough, the strategic bomber B-52 was inserted. It is said that the United States dropped more bombs over Vietnam—over North Vietnam and the battlefields in the south—than it dropped over all theaters of war in WWII: North Africa, Italy, Germany, and Japan. That the country didn't become a wilderness after this effort may be due to the fact that conventional bombing is only effective to a certain limit, a ruin can't become more than a ruin and that many bombs were missing the target, for instance, bombing jungle unoccupied by the guerrillas. The North Vietnamese air defense, for its part, was effective: anti-aircraft missiles (obtained from the Soviet Union, which in the middle of the 1960s began to replace China as supporting power) forced down the aircraft from high altitudes, and on lower altitudes, they became prey for everything from AA guns to handguns. Until December 1966 the US in Vietnam is said to have lost as many planes as it did in 1942 during WWII.

The situation in South Vietnam improved somewhat after the US deployed regular troops in 1965. But at the same time North Vietnam got bolder: from the beginning it had only supported the FNL guerrillas, for example by sending supplies via the Ho Chi-Minh-trail, going from North Vietnam via Laos and Cambodia to South Vietnam, but from the autumn of 1965, regular units of the North Vietnamese Army (NVA) were inserted in the south in parallel with the guerrilla. In particular, the guerrillas came to suffer rather high losses in the battles that followed, so that by the end of 1968 FNL was no longer a force to be reckoned with. But there were enough NVA units to keep the pressure up and by this time the American home front had turned against the war. So, to classify what kind of war this was, it wasn't an outright guerrilla war – no, from 1965 and on it was a *combined guerrilla and conventional war*. The operationally impossible situation for the United States was otherwise that enemy forces could come into South Vietnam from Laos or Cambodia, occupy a position that the Americans attacked and then sneak out again to Cambodia/Laos. As in the Battle of Dak To, 1967, covered by Atkinson (1989).

1968 was a turning point. In 1967 leading Americans thought they saw "light at the end of the tunnel". The FNL guerrilla had sustained losses and some formal, "ordinary" (as opposed to "total") victories against the NVA had been won. Then, on the new year of 1968, FNL launched a guerrilla offensive all over South Vietnam: concentrating on cities, NVA and guerrilla carried out strikes against military targets including the US embassy in Saigon, South Vietnam's capital. The Americans at home who could see everything on TV turned against the war virtually overnight. President Johnson promised a cease of Rolling Thunder and negotiations, while at the same time he said that he would not stand for another presidential period. The Vietnam war had broken him; the mental stress around every decision regarding this "small colonial war" had become too much for this son of Texas, comfortable with social issues and back-room negotiations but out of his depth in foreign policy matters.

The winner of the election of 1968, Richard Nixon, was more at home with a situation like this, though not even he could rectify the situation. Now, he had the aim of incrementally withdrawing the American troops and letting the South Vietnamese army do the fighting, supported by American weapons and US air force and naval air units. All through 1968, the fighting in South Vietnam was intense, army and Marines fighting the NVA, so intense that there was a brass shortage on the world market by this time; cartridges for handgun and artillery projectiles are made of brass. Now the United States had more than 500,000 men in Vietnam. But it wasn't enough to fight the circa 40 million population of North Vietnam.

The American C-in-C in Vietnam 1965-68 was the Virginian *William Childs Westmoreland* (1914-2005). His predecessor Harkins had through his reserved style annoyed journalists, these complaining that they never got to know anything. Westmoreland decided to change this, in particular by holding frequent press conferences and letting the correspondents rather freely roam the war zone; this was the opposite of the style of "embedding," later used. Thus, "Westy" believed he could win the press for the war effort but it wasn't to be: the press conferences became orgies in euphemisms which, coupled to TV teams filming dead and wounded American servicemen in the field, created a confidence gap between the war leadership and the people. Westmoreland had believed that the war would be won around 1968—but—since this was not to be he resigned and was replaced by *Creighton Abrams* (1914-1974), the armor commander previously mentioned in this book when relieving the paratroopers in Bastogne 1944. In Vietnam Abrams fought for a lost cause but at least in terms of media and communication, he was more restrictive with information. He had a more "operational" leadership style.

Nixon had intimated that the American commitment in Vietnam should be terminated. Units were sent home. But the battles continued, like invading Cambodia in 1970 to strike out the Communist ground force bases there. It seemed feasible operationally but the war-weary home front reacted against it with demonstrations and riots. So the option of only having South Vietnamese troops doing the fighting was the only left—and as intimated they were supported with American material and aircraft in large numbers, but to no avail. The moral of the South Vietnamese army had been low both before and after the Americans arrived. So, to make a long story short, the American commitment in Vietnam ended with the Paris peace of January 1973: all American ground units were sent home, only some air units staying behind. But in August the same year, Congress even banned all further use of American aircraft in the region.

The South Vietnamese would now on their own oppose the onslaught of NVA. Of course it wouldn't last. After a pause, the NVA in 1975 launched a conventional offensive with armor and artillery support and South Vietnam virtually fell apart by this avalanche. Faster than anticipated the Communists took Saigon and the US had to hastily evacuate its remaining embassy staff with helicopters landing on the roof of the Embassy. The helicopters then flew to an American aircraft carrier in the Gulf of Siam. This was in April 1975.

The Vietnam war couldn't be won like other COIN-operations after WWII (Malaya, the Philippines) because the guerrillas in Vietnam were supported by North Vietnam having a rather safe access to the south by way of Laos and Cambodia. NVA and FNL units could sneak into the south, attract the attention of American units, exchange fire in sometimes intense battles, and then sneak out again. To strategically combat such an enemy was a task of staggering dimensions, requiring the occupation of Laos and Cambodia too, and this no American policymaker seems to have had in mind when trying to get to grips with the Vietnamese problem.

Throughout this book, we've mentioned one line or two about pertinent equipment for every period – to give some symbolical depth, some vivid imagery to all the troop movements and decisions. And for the Vietnam War we can tell you this: the signature combat uniform color of US Army by this time was *olive green*, a rather grass-green hue.

19. H. NORMAN SCHWARZKOPF
(1934-2012)

URING THE CIVIL WAR, THERE was a Union force called *The Iron Brigade*. They had a mascot named "Old Abe," a bald eagle of a not uncommon American type. And this with time came to be the symbol of the 101st Airborne Division, *Screaming Eagles*, originating from this Iron Brigade. At this division, stationed in Fort Campbell, Kentucky, in 1957 the steadfast, bright, New Jersey born *Herbert Norman Schwarzkopf* arrived. He had chosen paratroopers after his West Point graduation, him being too large for tanks and the engineer corps not seeming exciting. By this time, however, the infantry and the army at large weren't so attractive. "Common knowledge" was that the air force would be at the front line of any future war, having the army only to clear out the resultant rubble. For the army of the 50s this meant that it mostly was equipped with WWII-style material, substantial renewal only beginning to set in by the 60s and 70s. By then, it was realized that you also needed an army to fight a modern war.

Schwarzkopf became a second lieutenant and trainer in an airborne ranger company. It was a backwater of a stationing, like Camp Swampy of the Beetle Bailey comic which began publishing by this time, the 50s. For instance, Schwarzkopf's company was commanded by an alcoholic, a man having served in WWII and failed in a civilian career and then having to return to the army, being forced to serve as an airborne ranger but himself being afraid to actually make those jumps out of an aircraft defining the service branch. He teased Schwarzkopf for having been to West Point, "that

139

tin soldier academy by the Hudson". But of course, you need to have some theoretical foundation in your officer life, like when planning exercises. So, in all, Schwarzkopf soldiered on, making the most of this stationing.

A few years later, in 1965, Schwarzkopf went to Vietnam as an adviser to the Army of the Republic of South Vietnam (ARVN). He was placed in a battalion of paratroopers, indigenous Vietnamese troops; Schwarzkopf had the honor to carry the 20-kg heavy radio of the battalion commander. One of the tasks was to be fire controller, calling for heavy support from mortars, artillery, and helicopters. He did indeed call for this kind of support during a massive patrol in the border region to Cambodia, a more than elementary lesson in the art of infantry warfare. It's all in his memoir, *It Doesn't Take a Hero*. Not all officers are in such an intense battle environment early in their career. True, this was Vietnam, a shooting war where many served, but as a career officer, there is indeed the possibility to choose assignments on HQs and facilities far away from the heat. Schwarzkopf, for his part, chose to be where the action was.

He was assigned to a unit of Vietnamese rangers. Due to its colonial past, the management language in Southern Vietnam was French. And Schwarzkopf happened to know this language, having learned it in school before West Point. This facilitated his getting this assignment. So let's look at the patrol he took part in as an adviser to the battalion commander (batcom), the big patrol intimated above.

In early July 1965, the FNL guerrilla besieged the ARVN camp Duc Co, located near the Cambodian border and just north of the Ia Drang river which was a focal point at this time. The camp had been set up to prevent guerrillas from crossing the border (the FNL had bases in Cambodia), but the camp had been surrounded and isolated during the summer, so now the surrounding area had to be cleared. The enemy was estimated to have two battalions there, around 700 men. According to the original plan paratroopers would be landed by helicopter in the wilderness 10 km northeast of Duc Co, and from there to the camp take a circumventing route clearing the ground from enemies. Attack aircraft would bomb the area in advance and during the whole operation bombers, artillery and a battalion of Vietnamese rangers in the town of Pleiku west of Duc Co would be available as support. All this sounded well—but—when Schwarzkopf went to Pleiku to speak with the responsible US headquarters to get it all confirmed, they said they had no aircraft available the next day which was D-Day. And artillery there was not, only one mortar in the surrounded camp with a maximum of 20 rounds left...! To top it all off it turned out that the designated landing zone was pure forest, not a clearing as believed. A new LZ was booked but it was on the other side of Duc Co, 24 km southeast of the camp. Also, the ranger battalion proved to be home on leave, impossible to gather in less than three days, so the whole grand plan was in shambles.

The plan had been a mere desktop product, created by a military adviser without battle experience. As elevated staff people, they didn't have to check all the facts, they would surely not be under fire during the operation; this was the role of Schwarzkopf and his battalion. Everything had to be canceled and recast. With a revised plan drawn up Schwarzkopf three days later could mount with his fellow rangers in forty UH-1's, holding ten soldiers each; they flew straight toward the camp, landed under enemy mortar-fire but could nonetheless get inside fairly unscathed. The camp itself was a triangle fenced by barbed wire, somewhat smaller than a football field. Schwarzkopf was met by a second lieutenant, the American camp adviser, who was delighted to have been relieved. But now it all began: the area would be cleared of enemies – so, the next day the newly arrived rangers left the camp to do this by roaming the terrain and checking it, opposing what guerrillas it did find, by first going north, then west towards the border, and then south-east to finally reach the camp again.

The unit strength was two battalions, partly the camp force and partly the new arrivals with Schwarzkopf and friends. They both now left camp, going in single file. In the afternoon, after 20 km was logged, gunfire was heard from the point, *la tête de la colonne*. They were now less than 8 kilometers from the Cambodian border.

Schwarzkopf with his radio called for helicopter gunship support whereby the threat was removed, the Gatling guns with its six 20 mm rotating barrels, firing 50 shots per second, providing effective support.

After the attack helicopters had done their job Schwarzkopf went to the point where three men had fallen. The bodies were shipped back with a transport helicopter Schwarzkopf previously had called to the scene to deliver ammunition. So the force continued its march. Once at the Cambodian border they camped, spending the night in the open with sentries posted so as not to be taken by surprise. Nothing happened during the night but there are countless stories from this war of patrols having frivolously neglected to put out guards and then being wiped out by a surprise attack. You have to expect the unexpected, in small battles and big ones – remember Shiloh, Kasserine, the Ardennes. In the morning they were off again with Schwarzkopf in the middle of the file; they worked their way south along the tangled jungle trails, the clock struck twelve – and then they were ambushed. Small arms fire and mortar hit them but the bamboo thicket was so dense that you couldn't "hit the dirt" – lie down on the ground for protection. The greenery was like a wall around them. But these Vietnamese rangers were tough guys who just stoically waited out the attack.

Now they had to get back to camp before the night, before the enemy had the time to group for an attack on the camp, threatening to eliminate it. But during the subsequent march, they were distracted by incessant ambushes, the jungle was as made for it, and each time Schwarzkopf had to call for airstrikes that cleared the terrain and then see if the coast was clear. But the batcom, Major Nghi, just wanted to hurry up and get to Duc Co as quickly as possible, this was better than to be 100% sure that the terrain was clear, so it ended up with him with his staff simply walking away from Schwarzkopf. He, therefore, joined the battalion who came last in the column.

After another assault, Duc Co was reached in the evening. The main force was safe but parts of the rear battalion were left out in the bush and were having difficulties to find its way back; this was relayed on the radio. At the same time, the soldiers in the camp feared an attack so they were easy on the trigger, anything moving in the forest could be shot at. Who would then be given the unpopular task of going out and leading the out-force back? Schwarzkopf, of course, and by radio and signal rockets the task was solved, the stranded unit was found and led home.

But the camp was still surrounded, 40 rangers had been killed and twice as many were wounded and air evacuation was precarious. But a Hercules aircraft soon arrived, landed and flew away with the wounded despite enemy fire. Then they sent out patrols supported by artillery observers in small Cessna aircraft to keep track of the besieging enemy; the fire was directed unto these troop concentrations. The camp was under mortar fire day and night, a well outside the camp could only be reached by combat patrols and food began to run out. After a week, however, rescue came in the form of Vietnamese marines advancing from the east. The enemy was eventually driven away by them, heading for the Cambodian border, and now it turned out that the first estimate of two Vietcong battalions was too modest; there had been two whole regiments of the NVA besieging Duc Co.

The whole affair was a temporary victory for the US supported side, but by the autumn North Vietnam continued to operate in the region, sending three NVA regiments down to South Vietnam's central highlands through Cambodia with the possible task to continue toward the coast and cut the country in half. Whether the NVA was able to reach this strategic level is uncertain, but the whole thing was a threat that the United States couldn't ignore; it now had regular troops in the land, setting the stage for the largest Vietnam battle thus far: the battle of Ia Drang Valley. It was the helicopter-borne 1st Cavalry Division who in November 1965 was sent to this valley south of Duc Co, still rather near the Cambodian border; it would be US Army's first encounter with the NVA, previously it had only fought against guerrillas. The unit was called Air Cav, harking back to the 7th Cavalry as mentioned earlier in this study, in the Custer chapter. When the battle was over, the Americans had managed to stop the offensive, if it were to be seen as such; maybe it was just a ruse in the form of the enemy attracting Americans to himself and then disappearing. However, in the aftermath of Ia Drang, all NVA units hadn't been able to get back to Cambodia, the secure base region, and the South Vietnamese paratroopers were now detailed to cut off their retreat. 2,000 men including Schwarzkopf were sent off, landed by helicopter and immediately gaining contact with the enemy. The valley had gotten its name from the Ia Drang River, flowing westward into Cambodia in a valley about 20 km wide. Here the enemies were supposed to be, retreating through the dense jungle to Cambodia and safety – for once in Cambodia they could either go to a nearby blue force camp or wander the Ho Chi Minh Trail to the north and eventually come to North Vietnam. The South Vietnamese brigade now took up positions on a hill south of the river, and the chief of staff, a colonel named Troung, planned to send out one battalion as a barrier in the west and one in the east, thus the enemy would be caught, and the brigade's two remaining battalions would be able to attack frontally after some prep fire by the artillery.

On D-Day, the flanking battalions were sent out and everything went as planned, oddly enough...! What you otherwise learn from the history of war is that elaborate plans like these almost always have to be revised during the battle, as Moltke once observed. Now NVA troops did exchange fire with the two battalions, with the western one at 8 o'clock and the eastern at 11 – and even this Troung had predicted, including the timing. The enemy was caught and he behaved as expected: after trying to flee to the west he turned to the east to find both roads blocked. After American prep fire lasting half an hour, called by Schwarzkopf, the two remaining battalions could make their frontal attack and when Schwarzkopf and Troung arrived at the scene in the afternoon they saw the enemy shattered by the fire. All told a unique example of how a plan, in fact, works out without disturbances, how an enemy really does behave as you expect him to do, otherwise a dangerous way to conceive of a battle.

This was the gist of Schwarzkopf's first tour of duty in Vietnam. During one operation he also got wounded, earning him a Purple Heart. He was a troop officer, he thrived in the challenges of combat. First, he went back to the States for some other assignments. Then he opted for a second Vietnam tour. In this process, he was promised the command of a US Army infantry battalion. But when he in 1969 actually was in Saigon at the actual HQ he was caught up in red tape. He might not get that command; instead, he could serve on a higher staff like this one, far from the action. But he said in no uncertain terms that he had been promised a battalion and that he should have it; he fought for his case. Other officers might just think, orders are orders, complying with the mission they get. Not Schwarzkopf, though, he wanted to have a troop command and soon got it: 1st Battalion, 6th Infantry, 198th Infantry Brigade at Chu Lai.

It was, however, something of a let-down for him when he saw the dismal state of the unit in question. To begin with, the helicopter he rides in is directed to the LZ by a not so soldiery type in a red bandanna.

This turns out to be one of the platoon leaders.

Schwarzkopf is then given a tour of the grouping. For instance, one sentry has a rusty machine gun, he has a transistor radio to wail away the time with – and a foxhole one decimeter deep. Schwarzkopf can't believe his eyes. He says to the sentry: "OK, let's practice. Take cover!" And, of course, the soldier can't take cover in that parody of a hole.

In the grouping, there are soldiers around not having helmets or weapons, they are unshaved and unkempt. When asking a company commander of the habit of not wearing helmets he says that they don't use them because their task is to... whereby Schwarzkopf interrupts, telling him not to teach *him* how to lead operations in the field.

As a scene out of military history this is great. It's like Patton coming to take over 2nd Corps in Djebel Kouif.

***

145

Schwarzkopf had gotten the worst battalion of the army on his lot. The enemy could practically walk straight into the camp, throw hand grenades and fire salvos with their Kalashnikovs and then disappear in the dark. So, a severe shake-up program was effected, inter alia by educating the junior officers. In general, they were freshmen, knowing that the draft loomed and thus in college choosing to be officers by way of ROTC (*Reserve Officer Training Corps*) to not end up as the lowliest grunt in Vietnam. But, according to Schwarzkopf, they lacked leadership qualities, they were merely a kind of corporals having by chance received a commission. Further, the battalion didn't have enough NCOs, the ones they had only having about 1-2 years of experience when 10-20 years is what is required for staffing a top notch-unit.

The battalion was placed in central Vietnam, just south of the border between North and South Vietnam – below the DMZ, *De-Militarized Zone*. Communist guerrilla and NVA were operating in the area and the task of the battalion was to prevent them from this. It was a policing mission, a territorial task in a war that couldn't be won since the enemy along with the North Vietnam territory had Cambodia as a base and Cambodia couldn't be attacked (and when Nixon finally did it in 1970 it created an outrage in the American public opinion). However, the battalion Schwarzkopf led soldiered on in its "counter-insurgence warfare" (COIN) as best as it could, like patrolling the countryside chasing guerrillas and intercepting gun caches. He did improve the standard of the unit, like having the soldiers always, any time equipped with helmet, weapon and bulletproof vest. It was like the Patton regime of tie, gaiters, and helmet in North Africa in 1942. In all, Schwarzkopf's work bore fruit; for instance, an intercepted enemy document estimated that a new battalion had taken over from the previous which was the best grade Schwarzkopf could get, a fine rating of his work indeed.

In 1970, his second service tour was over and Schwarzkopf went back to the States. After a stint in Washington he would attend Army War College; already in between his Vietnam tours he had attended the Command and General Staff School, essential for career advancement and becoming a general. In comparison to this, Army War College is a more leisurely school, very advanced in higher military and political education and, as such, another step to the top. The overall mood and atmosphere in the then US Army was shaped by the defeat in Vietnam; however, with time a material renewal program was brought into effect, resulting in hardware like the Abrams tank, the Bradley APC and Apache and Blackhawk helicopters, symbolizing a resurgence for the army and the US at large.

Schwarzkopf also served in troop assignments. One detail from one of these may be worth noting, when in 1974 being deputy commander of 172nd Infantry Brigade at Fort Richardson in Alaska. Though a strategic backwater, Schwarzkopf thrived in this wilderness, fishing and hiking in his spare time. The brigade commander, for his part, was a teetotaler and a devout Christian, insisting on the officers attending church every Sunday: good for morale, he thought. In any case, this commander also had the demand that every man, rankers and officers alike, must be able to run 5 miles in 50 minutes. This Latham fellow had seen soldiers in Korea being left behind just because of lack in physical strength so, like Liddell Hart said, every modern infantryman must be a ranger and an athlete.

After Alaska Schwarzkopf and his family (he was married to Brenda and they eventually had three kids) moved to the state of Washington in the north-west corner of the continental US. This was in 1976, Schwarzkopf at Fort Lewis being given the command of an infantry brigade, a unit with low morale which he in the usual fashion whipped up to the highest level. For this, he was promoted to Brigadier General. This brigade together with two other formed 9th Division, one of the ten first line infantry divisions US Army then had stationed at home in the USA. Plus six stationed overseas (one in Korea, one on Hawaii and four in West Germany) the army thereby had sixteen divisions in the first line, units with enlisted men because now conscription was history.

Additionally, there were independent brigades and battalions of the ranger and Special Forces kind, resulting in a total army strength of almost 800,000, with 500,000 stationed in the US and the rest overseas. The most important overseas force was the European Theater-army with over 200,000 men. Six of the stateside-stationed divisions also had their main supplies in Europe, whereby in the event of a conflict they could be deployed there rather fast by air. This was the Regular Army; then there was the National Guard as a reserve. In peacetime, the various National Guards were subsumed under each state respectively as emergency units, assisting during floods and storms etc. and even beating down riots, and in war they were intended as reinforcements to the army. The National Guard by this time had a strength of eight divisions and 25 brigades, constituting approximately 400,000 men. There was also an "army reserve" of support and maintenance units of about 200,000 men. With all these units, the army had a total strength of about 1.4 million men, and with the US Marines (four divisions, 200,000 men) the American ground force became even larger.

This was the US Cold War army, interesting to have as a pattern of how to organize an army by any time. And for contemporary US history, the pattern of Regular Army supported by the National Guard still applies.

***

In the late 70s, Schwarzkopf was sent overseas for a rather important assignment, namely as the deputy commander of a division in West Germany. To lead this 24,000 man unit in the focal point of the expected WWIII, of containing the imagined Red Army onslaught to the west, was a commanding task. A funny episode during this stationing was when Schwarzkopf noticed that the divisional helicopters weren't up to scratch, too many were on repair. The reason proved to be that the air battalion worked after an old norm, stating that it was enough to have 70% of the machines operational for "battle ready" status, while the new standard was no less than 75%. Norman then simply told the mechanics that now 75% is the standard – and lo and behold, soon there were more helicopters operational, the air battalion was deemed battle ready. For his part, the division commander was surprised at this, he wondered how Schwarzkopf had done it, had he taught the mechanics some new way to calibrate the turbines...? But, of course, there was no such thing involved, Schwarzkopf only told them to raise the bar.

Schwarzkopf's defining moment was as commander of the UN Alliance against Iraq in the Gulf War 1990-91. Focusing on operational details it can be said that the US had lost one valuable ally in the Middle East after the revolution in Iran in 1978. The US then put up a deployment force to be used in a new crisis, what eventually became Central Command which Schwarzkopf headed in 1990. The *casus belli* for it all remains a bit shady, Iraq may have been secretly goaded into taking Kuwait and then, as if by magic, giving the US the opportunity to strike back and "liberate" Kuwait. This writer has no proofs of this but with time he has come to doubt some of the official narratives of American history.

But as intimated in the Introduction, let's focus on operational details.

At the end of 1990, the UN Alliance (US, UK, French troops) had a substantial force grouped south of Kuwait and Iraq, some 500,000 men opposing an equal Iraqi force. Iraq, however, had more tanks, 5,500 to the 4,000 of the Alliance, but the Allies had more aircraft – a total of 1,850 to 550.

Then there was an air offensive – and then a ground attack, planned by Schwarzkopf. In this, there were minor forces binding the front of the Kuwait border (and the US Marines making amphibious landings on the coast as a diversion) while the main, armored assault of the Alliance was done on the left wing, starting west of Kuwait and penetrating well into Iraq, ending by the Euphrates after substantial damage done to Iraqi armor (Republican Guards) and everything else pertinent. So, while this writer does question the clear-cut official narrative, the generalship of Schwarzkopf in all this was not a bad performance. As a general he looked the part (six foot three) and he knew what combat was, what taking responsibility at the front meant. He headed for the most dangerous assignments, knowing that a tour of duty in Vietnam would be good for career advancement. In 1965, he could have stayed on as a West Point teacher and no one would have blamed him but it wouldn't have led him anywhere career-wise, this and other similar postings probably only giving him a decent service record and ending in a colonelship or so.

Instead, he headed for responsibility and, details aside, became a somewhat historical general. The Schwarzkopf figure has come to represent the archetype of "battlefield hero" like Patton and the other top names of this study. And he might even be the last such – in the US, maybe even in the world at large.

Herbert Norman Schwarzkopf was born in 1934 in New Jersey and had a father who was also general, of the same name, H. Norman Schwarzkopf, senior, but he never commanded troops in operations: a general without an army. He had served in the occupation forces in Germany after WWI and then as a military attaché. This function he inter alia held in Iran during WWII, having his son with him on this posting. Once father and son visited the Iranian central bank for some business, being shown down into the vault with all its crown jewels from the Safavids to Abbas the Great. Young Norman's look was captured by a globe in solid gold and with the seas made of emeralds, the land of rubies, and Iran itself with brilliants. Amazed he pointed at it and tried to say something to a banker who just said, "Oh that? That's just something we made of leftover jewels!"

***

An officer must be able to grasp the nettle and tell his men to do the same: *go get killed!* Conversely, he can't go around being nice. In the early 70s, when commanding that battalion in Vietnam, the soldiers once asked why the discipline was so rigorous, why they had to go around with helmet, gun and Kevlar vest all the time – and then Schwarzkopf explained it in terms of *c'est la guerre*, deal with it, operational demands being what they are, and he didn't mind if they liked it or not: "I'm not here to win a popularity contest!"

This rather well sums up the combat zone leadership persona.

20. MARGINALIA

UNDER THE CAPTION "Marginalia" we will here gather some aspects and reflections, stuff we haven't been able to subsume under the regular chapters of this book.

Anecdote

Here is an anecdote by courtesy of a US Army general. Since it isn't verbatim we won't provide the source. Anyhow, the officer was on his first Vietnam tour of duty as an adviser, being stationed in a jungle outpost manned by the South Vietnamese army. The post consisted of a helipad and a contingent of soldiers. The officer asked:

"Why is the outpost here?"

"To protect the landing site."

"And why is the landing site here?"

"To supply the outpost."

This is Vietnam *in nuce: we are here because we are here because we are here...*

US Navy

The US Constitution of 1789 said that the Republic should have both an army and a navy to defend it. We all know about the army by now, so how about the navy?

I don't know much about it. I only know that the US Navy in the Civil War formally served on the Union side. There we found Admiral Farragut, who in a sea battle was warned by his ADC that torpedoes were launched at them. To this, Farragut said:

"Damn the torpedoes! Full speed ahead!"

That's the warrior spirit in nuce, naval style.

We also see it in Pearl Harbor on 7 December 1941. That Sunday a naval chaplain was going to hold an outdoor service. Suddenly, Japanese planes were seen in the sky. The chaplain then grabbed a machine gun and fired at the planes with the lectern as support. This inspired the song, "Praise the Lord and Pass the Ammunition". This phrase, *per se*, was probably already around in the days of Oliver Cromwell, the puritanical, anti-royal rebel of the British 17th century.

Next, I have this regarding American naval realities. We often hear how magical it was when President Monroe launched his doctrine, that of wanting Europe to stay away from the New World. The US rules the New World, you others can rule the Old World. Okay, but how was this implemented, what was the actual force behind the words? Answer: the British Navy, world hegemony at the time. This is noted by Morison/Commager in *Growth of the American Republic* and it should be remembered by any student of history. The US and the UK have always maintained a special relationship.

In a magazine article in the 1970s, I read this about recruitment of US naval officers: they mustn't be ugly, like having facial blemishes and outstanding ears. Maybe this has to do with the navy being a sort of symbol of the US, its ships sailing around the world and its officers being the face of the Republic – if so, that face mustn't have any blemishes.

Serving on a ship, that's the core of the business. As a naval officer, you should aim at being the commander of a ship, even if it's just a torpedo boat. "Combat at sea" must be the lodestar for a naval officer. That's the *sine qua non* of a naval career. A TV series missing this was *JAG* when in one episode it had the "odd man out" in the context, Bud, having for the first time served as the prime defender in a military court case. After the event he was satisfied – but, hey, with all due respect, serving in court isn't what defines being in the navy. Being on a ship, on a mission defending the Republic, is.

So, in this respect, the TV series *The Winds of War* had a more sane approach. The main character, naval officer Pug, always speaks of wanting to command a ship. This captures the navy career *in* nuce.

Further: "We have seen the enemy – and he is ours." That's a saying of a US naval commander of the War of 1812, leading a unit on one of The Great Lakes. This, too, is the naval spirit in nuce.

Of course, if you are a naval lawyer such as we saw it in *JAG*, then do the best of it. Likewise, if you're into communications, do the best of it. A naval officer doing the best of his short career in the US Navy was Robert Anson Heinlein (1907-1988) – and his specialty was communications. He graduated from Annapolis with the class of 1929, became an officer and served on the carrier USS Lexington and the destroyer USS Roper. He had everything going for him, he had his dream job – and then he got pulmonary tuberculosis and was discharged on medical grounds. This was in 1934.

After a grey-area period of trying different jobs, he turned to writing. And rather quickly became a star of the science fiction genre. For instance, his knowledge of the military life, of the navy and of how to run a capital ship enabled him, with a little imagination added, to tell stories of space travel. Stories of responsibility, courage and even faith – faith in man, faith in the abilities of a young man learning to rise to the occasion.

Heinlein's novels have become classics, the novels about these aspects, of eternal values applied to the modern life, all in future clothing and setting. Novels like *Space Cadet* (1948), where it's said that an officer must be *a true and noble knight*. Novels like *Starman Jones* (1953) and *Time for the Stars* (1956) where the microcosm of the spaceship, out on long, dangerous journeys through uncharted territory, are well captured; the fantasy element of "future, space" is merged with a healthy sense of realism. Further, it is Heinlein's stories like *The Man Who Sold the Moon* (1950) and *Sixth Column* (1949) where the art of leading complex organizations is taught, the trick being to have a chief of staff at your side, this chief having a sizeable staff helping the leader to lead. Heinlein stresses how this system was created in Germany in the 19th century and this is a fine military wisdom to convey – in the context at hand, in popular stories, thus becoming an example of "serious fiction in popular form".

Heinlein could write many types of SF stories: juveniles, adventure, everyday realism. But the military man in him was a major source for stories and never is this better illustrated than in *Starship Troopers* (1959). It is about a future interstellar war against an alien species, with soldiers transported in ships and deploying for attack on enemy planets and asteroids. The realism of the naval life is there in portraying the ships and their routines, how they communicate and maneuver, and the ways of the infantry of the future – a kind of "Marines in space". To this, there's the political side, in the society portrayed the idea of public service being the prerequisite for the right to vote. Only persons having done public service have shown the responsibility for the society they live in.

In this scenario, any kind of public service counts, not just military service. But the gist of the novel is symbolically focused on military personnel being the flower of this society. Only military men can combine *responsibility with authority*, Heinlein means.

Heinlein was a unique voice. His brand of conservatism might seem now "standard American" and "the voice of the silent majority". But there wasn't many preaching what he did in the 50s and early 60s. Quite the contrary. Western world intellectuals by then played down the virtues of the West, instead hoping for socialism and mediocrity. Thus Heinlein, persistently advocating duty, honor, courage, and faith in man, and doing it in relatable stories, deserves all the praise he can get. He was an excellent representative of the US naval officer and of a man, period. This quote of him, criticizing specialization and instead lauding "the man of many talents," is very apt:

> A human being should be able to change a diaper, plan an invasion, butcher a hog, conn a ship, design a building, write a sonnet, balance accounts, build a wall, set a bone, comfort the dying, take orders, give orders, cooperate, act alone, solve equations, analyze a new problem, pitch manure, program a computer, cook a tasty meal, fight efficiently, die gallantly. Specialization is for insects. (from *Time Enough for Love*, 1973)

Archaic Strain

Walter Benjamin once said that *a modern city is characterized by its lack of monuments*, traditional monuments like statues. And this could be true of New York. The city is characterized by its buildings, deep street canyons, and bridges while designated monuments are scarce.

On the other hand, Washington has many statues and traditional monuments: Washington is archaic, New York is modern.

Even more in the realm of archaic monuments, we find in *Disneyland*, a place of idolatry if any. It is perfectly in order that it's an American dream to go there: *we're going to Disneyland* seems to be the watchword for the American dream vacation, yes, pilgrim journey – for even if it is kind of folksy and vulgar it doesn't rule out other forms of religious reverence existing in parallel, like in India where both the worship of a statue and meditation on the affinity between God and Man is contained within the same religion, conceptualized by Shankara in the 9th century.

The American equivalent to this would be: going to Disneyland in the morning, reading Thoreau's *Walden* at night.

As for American archaic strains like religion, we can also mention Marvel Comics, a naïve and therefore alive and viable god saga, at least up and until the early 80s. In comparison, European superhero comics (like *Camelot 3000*) never seem to take off. Superheroes are a natural American phenomenon, myths and legends indigenous to America. Also, George Lucas' Star Wars saga has the character of viable American myth, that which he said he was going to create. The basis of it in (American) Joseph Campbell's *The Hero with a Thousand Faces* tops it off.

A given archaic element in the US culture is the subject of this book, namely the *army*. And armies value traditions. *"War" stands for the archaic in the modern,* it has been said. A fine American example of this is the *Army War Flag* stored in West Point; it is a large silk flag with heraldic symbols and applied with bands inscribed with all the battles it has fought – all battles, not just victories which is the European practice in cases like these. Say what you like; the US Army War Flag flag has no modern function, it's a cry from the archaic.

An illuminating quote in the realm of "American archaic" is this by William Burroughs: "America is not the New World, it is immeasurably old, filled with death, consumed with the groveling worship of the Corn Goddess."

Atomic Saber

Nuclear weapons have been in the background in at least two American wars after WWII: Korea and Iraq. As we've seen, regarding Korea both MacArthur and Clark insisted on inserting them. And Eisenhower is said to have threatened the North with them if they didn't sign the cease-fire agreement. That may have been his "secret plan" he intimated during his presidential campaign. "I will go to Korea" and he did, in 1953, and the cease-fire was signed after this.

Mac has been called insane because he "rattled with the atomic saber". But, his fault was that he, in a general sense, seemed to be acting insubordinately towards Truman, the atomic dimension adding an ominous character to it all. Otherwise, all American leaders know that they can always use the atomic threat as a lever. Did the US use it to end the Iraq War in 1991? Iraqi secretary of state Tariq Aziz intimated as much in an interview.

War Books

Reading about American wars—what, then, to read?—The Bibliographical Note at the end of this book gives some clues to what sources I've used for it all. And implicitly, the book titles mentioned there are generally good reads too, foremost among them Yeager's memoirs, MacArthur's memoirs, William Marshall's *American Caesar*, d'Este's Patton bio, Ambrose's Eisenhower bio, Thomas' Lee bio, Wert's Custer bio and Fuller's *The Generalship of U. S. Grant*. And Sandburg's *Storm Over the Land*.

In this section, we will say something about other works worth reading: American war novels and essays.

My all-time favorite American war novel is *Bloody Beaches* by Delano Stagg (1959). On its 156 pages, it captures the gist of the Pacific War and maybe even war at large. Further, it has some human interest and psychological insight. For instance, the commander of the Marine company in question, Calvin Hobbes, is a careerist using his war service as a lever for his coming political career. While not excruciatingly profound as such, this feature gives the somewhat episodic narrative coherence.

"Episodic," I said... Actually, I kind of like the episodic character of *Bloody Beaches*. They invade diverse islands, from Guadalcanal to Iwo Jima, and each place becomes the scene of something different.

Over the years, this novel has lingered in my thoughts. Maybe it lacks this: tragedy. But, I say, better having a straightforward war story, well told, than a self-conscious story eager to prove how sensitive the author is and how much he hates war... and critics generally praise the latter kind, leading to Pulitzer awards and such. All told, *Bloody Beaches* is a gem, its author knowing what he talks about. I can't quote anything because the copy I read was in Swedish—but—believe you me, all along the way this novel has vivid imagery, authoritative facts and innovative settings of the operational kind.

Another story of the Pacific War is *Tarawa* by Tom Bailey. The Swedish edition I've consulted is 160 pages and has the endearing look of a dime-store novel, however, it is a factual rendition and I only mention it here for the record. The graphic design is great though, I love the cover and overall feel of this book. Again, this is "serious literature in popular form," if you enjoy reading of this particular operation (Tarawa / Betio of 1943) which of course was tough and hard-fought but not so interesting operationally. Mostly, it was a monotonous battering.

Moving on to the Korean War we find *Heartbreak Ridge* by Walker E. Blake, another dime-store novel, short and rather quaint. It is not sensationally good, not "Bloody Beaches good" but at least it starts in the combat zone with some general credibility in the storytelling. It is the "war of attrition, fixed lines" phase of the war, that is, operationally not so interesting. However, I'd rather read this than a thick-as-a-brick war novel supposedly being a classic.

Then, lastly, the Vietnam War. I've never encountered any novels from this war worthy of reading. No matter – for, instead, we have a couple of thick-as-a-brick essays, like *The Best and the Brightest* (Halberstam), *A Bright Shining Lie* (Sheehan) and *Vietnam – A History* (Karnow). The latter is okay, a traditional history, not sensational from a literary point of view; stylistically it might even be called "pedestrian". However, it does what it is supposed to, telling a historical tale (Vietnam from the beginning to our times) rather well.

As for Halberstam's book it is too long, too indulgent, on every turn of the road (of the US becoming engaged in Vietnam) implicitly asking, "is this where it went wrong, where the greatest land in the world became embroiled in a costly war ending in defeat"...?

(As a side note, a better book by Halberstam is *The Fifties,* a less programmatic, more readable account of odd and maybe not so odd personalities of that decade, the American 50s.) The same indulgent attitude may linger beneath the surface of Sheehan's Vietnam book, *A Bright Shining Lie.* However, it has the advantage of focusing the narrative on one person, John Paul Vann, an army officer first serving as military advisor to the South Vietnamese army in 1962-63, then ending his military career, then returning to Vietnam as a civil advisor. He died in a helicopter crash there in 1972. With all the industry, cunning, frustration and tragedy he embodies he is a rather fine symbol of the US engagement in Vietnam.

Sheehan's book isn't essential reading but it has its overall qualities, in composition, style, and knowledge of its subject, the Vietnam War.

The last among the overly thick Vietnam books I've read is Rick Atkinson's *The Long Gray Line: The American Journey of West Point's Class of 1966.* Well researched, with "human interest" and scenes of tough jungle combat, this book depicts the West Point Class sustaining the highest losses during the war. Also, it has scenes of peripheral stuff that might or might not be interesting. Lastly, there is the episode of the building and inaugural of the Washington monument over the war (the angular slab with names of Vietnam war deaths inscribed, plus the heroic statue towering above it). This kind of brings closure to the story.

As for pro and con about thick, 1000+ pages works, that which I've intimated I don't like, it might of course sometimes be that the stuff you're telling about tends to run up the page count. And it might not be a bad thing per se. However, I personally am not so enthusiastic about reading these bricks of books nowadays, be they novels or essays.

Thus, focusing on shorter Vietnam books I can fully recommend Robert Mason's *Chickenhawk,* the autobiography of a combat helicopter pilot (OK, it wasn't so short, it was over 500 pages...). The back cover blurb had the line, "the fear and belligerence, the mixed emotions of a chickenhawk" – and this captures the gist of flying the

Bell "Huey" chopper, an army transport helicopter both giving you a feeling of might *and* being vulnerable to hostile machine gun fire. The book illuminates the whole war from a modest perspective, that of a helicopter pilot. This book has no bullshit jargon, no posing, no "look at me, I'm writing a profound book of war". The praise given to this book is fully justified.

Also, among the shorter Vietnam works, we have Michael Herr's *Dispatches*, stylistically high-profile and a bit "over the top" as such, but it has its moments. Like noting the beauty of a Douglas AC-47 "Gunship" peppering a hill of Khe Sanh 1968 with tracers. It's like d'Annunzio appreciating the cathedral of Reims in flames in 1915. "War is good for you" – a reckless but at times true statement, in the alchemy of war, life, and death.

The book you're reading is focusing on army generals, the war on land. However, as intimated in the introduction some air force generals are brought along too, covering the war in the air, and a fine book exploring the world of the 50s armed forces pilot is *The Right Stuff* (1979). The main subject of the book is the space program of Project Mercury but since the seven astronauts of it were recruited from the cadres of the air force and navy pilots the author Tom Wolfe takes some time to picture the dangerous, macho world they lived in.

Dangerous: the striving male of those times may have spoken about the "murderous competition" in their civilian, corporate careers – but – the armed forces pilot of the 50s could with more justification say that their business *was* murderous indeed. Flying supersonic jet planes is always risky and it was even more dangerous in those pre-computer, not-so-advanced avionics days.

So, the armed service's pilots got used to attending funerals of their comrades, having been "killed in action" in the peacetime duty of flying jets.

And in that world of being a crack pilot, the top man was Charles Yeager, the man breaking the sound barrier in 1947 (q.v. Chapter Sixteen). Wolfe portrays that flight in his book as well as his 1963 attempt at breaking the flight altitude record with the specially equipped Starfighter, again covered in Chapter Sixteen. Sandwiched in between those is the story of the Mercury astronauts recruited from that crack pilot milieu, in the long run giving the US the know-how to go to the moon. Project Mercury managed to take the lead in the space race over Soviet Russia which from 1957-61 was the first in launching a satellite and putting a man in orbit.

All told, Wolfe's book was a beacon of heroism in a stale, late 70s culture all but given up on ever painting such rousing pictures about the post-war world. For this, *The Right Stuff* deserves eternal praise. The introduction covering Yeager's 1947 record attempt is great, his later altitude record attempt also – and the bulk of the book, the story of the Mercury astronaut, is fine too, non-ironically presenting us with heroes going up there to risk their lives for the glory of mankind. The style is that of "new journalism," giving factual reporting a kind of literary edge. In this, there is sometimes the risk of ending up in empty jargon or even in pedestrian, anecdotal reporting, however, on the whole Wolfe carries the day. He credibly painted a heroic picture that even became a rather fine, eponymous film in 1983.

The Right Stuff is the stuff that legends are made of.

Films

This writer has seen many films portraying American wars. But – he won't spend time telling you about all of them. The bad ones will simply be ignored. Instead, he will concentrate on three he really enjoyed. They all happen to be about the Vietnam war.

The best film to come out of this American experience is Francis Coppola's *Apocalypse Now* (1979). It lives in a curious borderland of myth and fact, of "stuff made up" and reality. I can only bow to the script writing abilities of John Milius and Coppola's casting and directing talent. In this film, all came together beautifully. Details aside, it takes the quest story of Joseph Conrad's "imperialism novel" *Heart of Darkness* and places it in Vietnam, making the aim of the riverboat trip the capture of a renegade Special Forces officer. The trip serves to line up diverse characters and scenes, each capturing some aspect of the war – foremost of these being Robert Duvall's Lieutenant Colonel Bill Kilgore. Here we have the slightly mad, over the top, larger than life character of the American officer in the field, the Patton style perilously transformed to Vietnam, so to speak.

The storytelling of this film is endearingly free. There might be a sense of drama and tragedy permeating it all but the film doesn't try too hard to convey this. "Tight but loose" describes the work rather well.

And then the denouement at the jungle temple where Kurtz (played by Marlon Brando) is opposed by the hero, the government agent in the form of Martin Sheen. It is all a masterful ambiguity, a successful attempt at myth-making in a 20th century setting. It is *the modern* (the 1960s historical framework) ending up in *the archaic*, in the form of the temple ruin in the jungle being Kurtz's base.

Thus, when knowing that you can always return to this film (and its quotes, and its soundtrack, mixing suggestive synth music with Wagner and The Doors), you don't have to be too harsh on a Vietnam film issued the year before it: Michael Cimino's *Deer Hunter* (1978).

And even on its own terms, this is a great work, being a film in the tradition of *great acting and tragedy* – believable tragedy. It is about going to war in Vietnam and experiencing hell. In this, in the Vietnam part of the film (the middle part), the element of "VC playing Russian roulette with American POWs" might be fictitious as such but it conveys a real sentiment, that of a bitter war. It symbolically sums up the war efficiently.

All told, sometimes Hollywood could excel, even in the process of somewhat industrial filmmaking – like, in this case, having a long process of scriptwriting, resulting in a script kind of "designed by committee" but coming out right in the end.

The best Vietnam-themed film of the 80s might be *First Blood* (Kotcheff 1982). A Special Forces veteran is hiking around in the States after the war, becoming harassed by a police officer and then driven too far, starting a one-man war against the Establishment / the Government / the State / the Man, it all taking place in a desolate backwoods region and thus allowing the hero to use his SF super soldier skills. This is both a crowd-pleasing action story, like a modern Western *and* emotionally believable. The hero awakens our sympathy in a natural way. There is some elegance in the scenario of, "you, Uncle Sam trained me into this super soldier; now, when you oppose me, pay the price". That the sequels weren't as genuinely great doesn't diminish the stature of this film, *First Blood.*

Finally, a look at *We Were Soldiers* (Wallace 2002), another wholly commendable work about Vietnam. It is a film about soldiers doing what soldiers are supposed to do: engage in lethal combat, fight and kill, fight and die. It is about the Battle of Ia Drang in 1965 where several US Army Air Cav battalions engaged a possibly superior North Vietnamese force.

Details aside, it is an heroic tale, maybe the only Vietnam film thus far with this attitude, partly enabled by the Ia Drang battle being a US victory, coming as it did rather early in the war (1965). And in this pattern, Mel Gibson as Colonel Hal Moore comes through as a credible battlefield hero.

The Image of the General

When I say, "image of the general" I here mean it in the leadership way. How did the American generals lead, how shall we imagine us them in the thick of battle?

For the record, it can be said that even though this book aims at portraying "battlefield commanders," no general doing his business stood exactly in the frontline drawing fire on himself. That's not what a general should do. That's the task of privates, squad and platoon leaders and company commanders. Already at the battalion level, it becomes more secure – even though, as we saw *batcom* Hal Moore in the *We Were Soldiers* film just mentioned, had his share of dangerous moments in the Ia Drang battle. It was a fiction film but based on real events.

But a commanding general is not to compare with a battalion or regimental commander. A general should lead efficiently and not brave danger unnecessarily.

Let's look at Norman Schwarzkopf in this respect. As intimated he represented the archetype of the "battlefield hero". And in Vietnam, he attended the school of lethal combat. However, for the sake of historical imagery, the Gulf War he led from the basement of a hotel in Riyad. He wasn't out riding a tank or a helicopter. There is, of course, a thing called "tactical HQ" which needs tanks and choppers for doing its duty. But that's for leading divisions and brigade battle groups, not armies.

In the Battle of Saratoga Benedict Arnold was a subordinate general. At one time, he took a horse and rode to the front line, the place of decision. That was a "Napoleonic" move, you might say, a thing you could do in the era of the *musket*. However, in the subsequent era of the *rifle* the front line, the danger zone, "where the metal meets the metal," became too dangerous for generals to even visit. "Go back, General Lee, go back!" is a quote from a Civil War battle where Lee wanted to have a look at the action but was told to stay away. Lee was of more use some hundred meters back, behind the lines commanding than being shot at. Then, of course, the general mustn't be too far off from the action. He mustn't hide in a dugout, like Fredendall in North Africa 1942. Or U. S Grant, being 10 km away from Shiloh when that battle began.

Oddly enough, the probably best American general of WWII, Douglas MacArthur, once got the nickname "Dugout Doug". That was during and after the Philippines, I guess. However, later in the war, his image approved, partly by having pictures of him and his HQ wading ashore at Pacific islands, giving the impression of a general leading from the front. However, even Mac was once stopped from actually visiting the front line by a stern sentry. I guess William Marshall told of this. Top generals have no business being in the combat zone proper.

A general leading a battle should be in a kind of focus, close enough to get the feel of the battle and knowing what's happening.

However, the actual hand-to-hand fighting is best left to the fighters. Then you can say, Alexander the Great, Caesar and Charles XII actually took part in melees. But that was their bent of nature. "Go all the way, then step back" is a better watchword for the field commander.

BIBLIOGRAPHICAL NOTE

IT'S A DAY IN FEBRUARY 2018 when I sit down to write this "bibliographical note" – some facts regarding my sources.

For general facts, I've used diverse encyclopedias, summaries, and overviews. Otherwise, for each chapter, my notable sources are these (see literature list for details about each book). For general guidance on the subjects the praise goes to these authors; the blame, should I have misunderstood something, goes to me.

For the Lee chapter, the main source is Emory M. Thomas *Robert E. Lee.*

The anecdote of Meade receiving a messenger in his camp, bringing his appointment to the command of the Army of the Potomac, is from Carl Sandburg's *Storm Over the Land.*

The main source of the Grant chapter is J. F. C. Fuller's *The Generalship of Ulysses S. Grant.*

The main source of the Jackson chapter is Frans G. Bengtsson's essay about the man in *Litteratörer och militärer.* Bengtsson's essay on Grant in *Silversköldarna* has supplied some info to the McClellan chapter.

T. Harry Williams' *McClellan, Sherman, and Grant* is a succinct essay having given me some angles for the chapters concerned.

Jeffery D. Wert's *Custer* is the main source of the Custer chapter.

Frank E. Vandiver's *Black Jack: The Life and Times of John Pershing* is the main source of the Pershing chapter.

The main source of the Marshall chapter is Ed C. Cray's bio.

The sources of the MacArthur chapter are *American Caesar* by William Manchester and Michael Schaller's *Douglas MacArthur: The Far Eastern General*. And MacArthur's own memoirs.

The sources of the Patton chapter are the bios by Whiting and D'Este, the latter entitled *Patton – A Genius for War*.

The main source of the Eisenhower chapter is Stephen E. Ambrose's *Eisenhower*.

The main source of the Bradley chapter is the man's autobiography, *A Soldier's Story*.

The main source of the Chennault chapter is *Flying Tigers* by Paul Szuskiewitch.

The main source of the Doolittle chapter is Ted W. Lawson's *Thirty Seconds Over Tokyo*.

The facts about weapons in the Groves chapter are mainly from Frederick Myatt's *Small Arms*. The info about various rations are from Bauer's book.

The main source of the Yeager chapter is his autobiography, written by him and Leo Janos.

The main source of the Korea chapter is Callum MacDonald's *Korea – the War Before Vietnam*. The info about the first onslaught of T-34 tanks at the start of the war is from Halberstam's *The Fifties*.

If I should mention one source of the Vietnam chapter it would be Stanley Karnow's *Vietnam – A History*.

The main source of the Schwarzkopf chapter is his autobiography, *It Doesn't Take a Hero*. The info about the divisional organization is from the Swedish army publication *Arménytt*.

LITERATURE

Magazine Articles

ANONYMOUS: "Amerikansk divisionsorganisation" in Arménytt 1/1979

ANONYMOUS: "Amerikanska armén" in Arménytt 2/1982

Books

AMBROSE, Stephen E. *Eisenhower: Soldier, General of the Army, President-Elect (1893-1952)*. I. New York: Simon & Schuster 1983

AMBROSE, Stephen E. *Eisenhower: The President (1952-1969)*. II. New York: Simon & Schuster 1984

ATKINSON, Rick. *The Long Gray Line: The American Journey of West Point's Class of 1966*. Boston: Houghton Mifflin 1989

BAILEY, Tom: Tarawa. Stockholm: Wennerbergs 1964

BAUER, Eddy. *Mannen i ledet*. Höganäs: Bokorama 1981

BENGTSSON, Frans G. "Stonewall Jackson" in *Litteratörer och militärer*. Stockholm: P. A. Norstedt & Söners förlag 1929

BENGTSSON, Frans G. "Ulysses S. Grant" in *Silverskölddarna*. Stockholm: Albert Bonniers förlag 1931

BLAKE, Walker E. *Heartbreak Ridge*. New York: Monarch 1962

BRADLEY, Omar N. *A Soldier's Story.* New York: Holt Publishing Co. 1951

CRAY, Ed C. *General of the Army: George C. Marshall, Soldier and Statesman.* Norton 1990

D'ESTE, Carlo. *Patton: A Genius for War.* New York City: Harper Collins 1995

FELLMAN, Michael. *Citizen Sherman: A Life of William Tecumseh Sherman.* New York: Random House 1995

FULLER, J. F. C. *The Generalship of Ulysses. S. Grant.* London: J. Murray 1929

GRAMM, Kent. *Gettysburg: A Meditation on War and Values.* John Wiley & Sons 1998

HALBERSTAM, David. *The Best and the Brightest.* New York: Random House 1972

- *The Fifties.* New York: Ballantine Books 1993

HARGREAVES, Reginald. *Great Land Battles.* London: The Hamlyn Publishing Group Ltd 1972

HEINLEIN, Robert A. Sixth Column. New York: Gnome Press 1949

- Space Cadet. New York: Scribner 1948

- Starman Jones. New York: Scribner 1953

- Starship Troopers. New York: Putnam 1959

- The man Who Sold the Moon. Chicago: Shasta 1950

- Time for the Stars. New York: Scribner 1956

HERR, Michael. *Dispatches.* New York: Knopf 1977

HIRO, Dilip. *Desert Shield to Desert Storm: The Second Gulf War.* Abingdon-on-Thames: Routledge 1992

KARNOW, Stanley. *Vietnam: A History.* London: Penguin Books, 1991

LAWSON, Ted W. *Thirty Seconds Over Tokyo.* Dulles, Virginia: Brassey's Inc., 2003 (60th anniversary reprinted edition)

MACARTHUR, Douglas. *Reminiscences of General of the Army Douglas MacArthur.* Annapolis: Bluejacket Books 1964

MACDONALD, Callum. *Korea – the War Before Vietnam*. London: MacMillan 1986

MANCHESTER, William. *American Caesar: Douglas MacArthur, 1880-1964*. New York: Little, Brown & Co. 1978

MASON, Robert. *Chickenhawk*. London: Penguin Books 2005

MYATT, Frederick. *Small Arms: An Illustrated Encyclopedia of Famous Military Firearms from 1873 to the Present Day*. London: Tiger Books International 1989

MORISON, Samuel Eliot, and Commager, Henry Steele. *The Growth of the American Republic*. New York: Oxford University Press 1951

SANDBURG, Carl. *Storm Over the Land*. 1942

SCHALLER, Michael. *Douglas MacArthur: The Far Eastern General*. New York: Oxford University Press 1989

SCHWARZKOPF, H. Norman. *It Doesn't Take a Hero: The Autobiography of General H. Norman Schwarzkopf*. New York: Bantam Books 1993

SHEEHAN, Neil. *A Bright Shining Lie*. New York: Vintage Books 1988

STAGG, Delano. *Bloody Beaches*. Falun: B. Wahlströms Bokförlag, 1979 (orig. 1959)

SZUSKIEWITCH, Paul. *Flying Tigers*. 1986

THOMAS, Emory M. *Robert E. Lee: A Biography*. New York: W. W. Norton & Co. 1995

VANDIVER, Frank E. *Black Jack: The Life and Times of John J. Pershing*. College Station: Texas A&M University 1977 (two volumes)

WERT, Jeffrey D. *Custer: The Controversial Life of George Armstrong Custer*. New York: Simon & Schuster 1996

WHITING, Charles. *Patton*. New York: Ballantine Books 1971

WILLIAMS, T. Harry. *McClellan, Sherman and Grant*. New York: Ivan R. Dee Publishers 1991

WOLFE, Tom. *The Right Stuff*. New York: Farrar, Straus & Giroux 1979

COMMANDERS

YEAGER, Charles and Janos, Leo. *Yeager: An Autobiography.* New York: Bantam 1985

INDEX OF PERSONS

BRADLEY, Omar N.   40, 77-78, 81, 91-95, 127, 147

BRANDO, Marlon   164

CHENNAULT, Claire Lee   97-101

CIMINO, Michael   164

COPPOLA, Francis Ford   163

CUSTER, George A.   47, 49-54, 74, 127, 144, 159

DOOLITTLE, James H.   6, 66, 103-109

DUVALL, Robert   164

EISENHOWER, Dwight D.   61, 74-75, 77-78, 80, 85-86, 88, 95, 158-159

GRANT, Ulysses S.   16-17, 22-38, 44, 46, 75, 78, 86-87, 115, 159, 166

GROVES, Leslie   111-112, 116-117

HEINLEIN, Robert A.   155-156

JACKSON, Thomas "Stonewall"   10, 12, 14, 36-37, 39-41, 86-87

COMMANDERS

LEE, Robert E.   6, 9-18, 21, 23, 33-37, 40-41, 45, 50, 75, 87, 97, 133, 159, 166

LINCOLN, Abraham   12-13, 16-17, 21-22, 28, 30-31, 33, 35, 44-46, 49, 54, 68, 78

MACARTHUR, Douglas   15, 40, 46, 58, 63-65, 68-69, 71-72, 88, 114, 117, 126-129, 158-159, 166

MARSHALL, George C.   58-61, 72, 79, 85, 88, 116, 159, 166

MEADE, George G.   11, 15-16, 19-22, 29

MCCLELLAN, George B.   9, 11, 13, 22, 34, 36-38, 43-46, 55, 105

MONTGOMERY of Alamein   46

PATTON, George S.   15, 58, 73-83, 92, 94-95, 115, 126, 133, 145-146, 150, 159, 164

PERSHING, John J.   55-56, 58-59

ROOSEVELT, Franklin D.   60, 65, 67-68, 78

ROOSEVELT, Teddy   54, 57

SCHLIEFFEN, Alfred von   11

SCHWARZKOPF, H. Norman   139-150

SHEEN, Martin   164

SHERMAN, William T.   17, 28-29, 32-34, 36, 38, 64, 75, 81, 86, 115

ABOUT THE AUTHOR

LENNART SVENSSON (1965-) is a Swede mostly writing in English. Notable works are *Ernst Jünger – A Portrait* (2014), *Science Fiction Seen From the Right* (2016) and the self-help guide *Actionism – How to Become a Responsible Man* (2017). In 2018 he published a war novel playing on the Eastern Front of WWII, *Burning Magnesium*.

www.ingramcontent.com/pod-product-compliance
Lightning Source LLC
Chambersburg PA
CBHW021403090426
42742CB00009B/975